# Bridging the Race and Gender Gaps
Representation of Women andMinorities among
MacArthur Fellows, 1981-2018

Adonis & Abbey Publishers Ltd

St James House
13 Kensington Square,
London, W8 5HD
United Kingdom

Website: http://www.adonis-abbey.com
E-mail Address: editor@adonis-abbey.com

Nigeria:
Suites C3 – C6 J-Plus Plaza
Asokoro, Abuja, Nigeria
Tel: +234 (0) 7058078841/08052035034

Copyright 2021 © Amadu Jacky Kaba

British Library Cataloguing-in-Publication Data
A catalogue record for this book is available from the British Library

ISBN: 9781913976040

The moral right of the author has been asserted

All rights reserved. No part of this book may be reproduced, stored in a retrieval system or transmitted at any time or by any means without the prior permission of the publisher

# Bridging the Race and Gender Gaps
## Representation of Women and Minorities among MacArthur Fellows, 1981-2018[1]

Amadu Jacky Kaba

---

[1] Parts of this book appeared in: Kaba, Amadu Jacky. 2020. "MacArthur Fellows, 1981-2018: Gender, Race and Educational Attainment," *Sociology Mind*, 10, (2): 86-126.

Dedicated to Andzi, Fudia and Mahan

# Table of Contents

**Dedication** .................................................................................................. v

**Chapter One**
Introduction ............................................................................................ 9

**Chapter Two**
Conceptualizing Genius and Creativity ............................................ 15

**Chapter Three**
Methodology ........................................................................................ 21

**Chapter Four:**
Findings/Results .................................................................................. 27

Table 1. Sex/Gender and Racial Breakdowns of MacArthur Fellows, 1981 to 201819 ..................................................................... 28

Table 2. State/Country and Region of Birth of MacArthur Fellows, 1981 to 2018, by Sex and Race
................................................................................................................ 32

Table 3a. First Names of MacArthur Female Fellows, 1981 to 2018
................................................................................................................ 41

Table 3b. First Names of MacArthur Male Fellows, 1981 to 2018
................................................................................................................ 48

Table 4. Age at Time of Award of MacArthur Fellows, 1981 to 2018
................................................................................................................ 58

Table 5. Year at Time of Award of MacArthur Fellows, 1981 to 2018
................................................................................................................ 61

Table 6. U.S. State, U.S. Region, Country, and World Region Where MacArthur Fellows were Located at the Time of Award, 1981 to 2018 ........................................................................................................ 64

Table 7. Earned Highest/Terminal Higher Education Degree of MacArthur Fellows, 1981 to 2018, by Sex and Race ...................... 70

Table 8. Alma Mater of Earned Highest/Terminal Higher Education Degree and type of Degree of MacArthur Fellows, 1981 to 2018, by Sex and Race ........................................................................................ 76

Table 9. Year of Graduation of for Earned Highest/Terminal Higher Education Degrees of MacArthur Fellows, 1981 to 2018, by Sex and Race................................................................................. 94

**Chapter Five**
**Discussion** ...............................................................................................99

**Chapter Six**
Conclusion ...............................................................................................117

**References** ............................................................................................115

**Appendices** ..........................................................................................125

**Index** ....................................................................................................129

# CHAPTER ONE

## Introduction

One of the most important contributing factors for advanced or developed societies or countries to have the status or prestige they enjoy today is the productivity (scientific and cultural) of their colleges, universities, research institutes and centers. One can safely claim that a society's progress or advancement is correlated to the quality and quantity of its higher education institutions. Research by Kaba (2012a) of the 2009 *Times Higher Education* top 200 ranked universities in the world shows that 54 (27%) were located in the United States; 29 (15%) in the United Kingdom; 11 (5.5%) each in Canada, Japan, and the Netherlands; 10 (5%) in Germany; and 9 (4.5%) in Australia (p.9). These are also among the nations with the largest GDP and GDP per capita in the World. Their ranked universities tend to have the largest endowments in the world. For example, Kaba's (2012a) study found that the combined endowment of all eight Ivy League universities (Brown University, Cornell University, Dartmouth College, Columbia University, Harvard University, Princeton University, University of Pennsylvania, and Yale University), ranked in the 2009 Times Higher Education top 200 universities in 2007, was $98.7 billion (p.28). To put this in context of how substantial this total endowment of these universities is, as of December 17, 2018, the World Factbook lists 230 nations and entities based on their 2017 gross domestic product. The $98.7 billion combined endowment of all eight Ivy League institutions in 2007 would rank number 86, below Croatia ($102.1 billion), ranked number 85, and above Côte d'Ivoire ($97.1 billion), ranked number eighty-six.

Students or their families and governments of societies where those higher education institutions are located are primarily responsible for funding higher education. Besides, philanthropic organizations such as foundations make significant contributions in supporting the education and research of those who are enrolled or work at colleges and universities. Some of the largest or wealthiest foundations are international in their giving, while others are more nationally or domestically focused. The vast majority of foundations provide grants, meaning that a person, group or entity must apply, wait for a decision, and if the decision is yes, a report is usually required to provide a summary of the project. Some foundations, on the other hand, can provide a no strings attached support to individuals or organizations. In such an instance, the recipient of the award, grant or fellowship is not aware whether their name is submitted for such an award. Internationally, the Nobel Memorial Prize is an example of an award that comes with a substantial amount of money and gold medal, where the recipient does not apply (Zuckerman, 1992; Wallerstein, 2002). Nationally, in the United States, the MacArthur Fellows Program is an example of no strings attached money of over $600,000 awarded annually to dozens of talented individuals from all walks of life during a five year period to be used whichever way they wish to help them in their academic research or artistic creations.

The MacArthur Fellows Program was established in 1981 by the MacArthur Foundation. According to the MacArthur Foundation: "The MacArthur Fellowship is a 'no strings attached' award in support of people, not projects. Each fellowship comes with a stipend of $625,000 to the recipient, paid out in equal quarterly installments over five years." The Foundation also adds that the Fellows Program intends: "to encourage people of outstanding talent to pursue their own creative, intellectual, and professional inclinations. … Recipients may be writers, scientists, artists, social scientists, humanists, teachers, entrepreneurs, or those in other fields, with or without institutional affiliations. They may use their fellowship to advance their expertise, engage in bold new work, or, if they wish, to change fields or alter the direction of their careers." ("About MacArthur Fellows Program," 2019; also see Coutu, 2007; "MacArthur Fellows Program: Summary of 2012-2013 Review," 2013; Wallerstein, 2002; Ward, 2001; Zuckerman, 1992: 218). There are two terms or words that the public, especially the media have used to identify the MacArthur Fellows Program: "Genius" and "Creativity". The public almost always refers to the Fellows Program as the 'Genius' award, while some, including the MacArthur Foundation itself, refers to the word "creative" or "creativity" to discuss the Program.

There have been numerous published scholarly peer-reviewed journal articles, books, public intellectual articles in periodicals, dissertations, and newspaper articles combined, focusing on various aspects of the backgrounds of MacArthur Fellows. Most of these publications focus on the profiles or backgrounds of the Fellows (Cox and Daniel, 1984; Von

Gunten, 2009; Moritz, 1998; Pais, 2011; Powell, 2008; Schimke, 2016). Others focus on the history and characteristics of the MacArthur Fellows Program (Coutu, 2007; Ward 2001; Zuckerman, 1992). Some of these publications also focus on the impact of the Fellows Program on the Fellows' careers (Powell, 2008; Rocca, 2017; Schimke, 2016; Silka, 2014), while others tend to criticize various aspects of the Program, including the selection method (Benzon, 2018; Kinsley, 1981; Rocca, 2017: 85; Wooster, 2010). For example, according to Rocca (2017), the MacArthur Fellows Program was "… created to correct for the perceived alienation of genius in American culture, [but] it tended to produce yet more alienation" (p.85). From 1981 to 2018, a total of 1,014 individuals have been selected as MacArthur Fellows. It is noted that out of "…2,000 people nominated each year, between 20 and 25…" receive the Fellowship (Schimke, 2016: 38).

The MacArthur Foundation has also published several studies and reports on the MacArthur Fellows Program, focusing on the backgrounds of the Fellows and the success of the Program (MacArthur Fellows: The First 25, 1981-2005; "MacArthur Fellows Program: Summary of 2012-2013 Review," 2013; "Review Affirms Impact and Inspiration," 2013). One such publication presents data on the undergraduate alma maters of all the Fellows (Conrad, 2017). Another study focuses on the place of birth of the Fellows ("Fellows Location at Birth," 2018). Another study focuses on the U.S. state or country where a Fellow was located when they won the award ("Fellows Location at Award," 2018). This current study will build on the research findings or results of a number of these publications.

One important limitation of the various publications mentioned above on the MacArthur Fellows Program is that none of them examined the gender and racial/ethnic breakdowns, and the terminal or highest academic degrees earned by all of the Fellows. A study containing such findings will make a significant contribution to the understanding of the types of people receiving these fellowships. This information is very important especially in a country as diverse as the United States. In addition, women and minorities have made significant progress in the society especially from the 1990s to present. It is usually through an organization such as the MacArthur Fellows Program that the public becomes aware of women and minorities who have made significant contributions to society. For most of these Fellows, the public did not know them or aware of them until their selection by the MacArthur Fellows Program.

This study examines the backgrounds of MacArthur Fellows for the almost four-decade period from 1981 to 2018. This is done by focusing on the gradual progress that women and minorities have made in almost all sectors of American society. This progress may be reflected by the annual increase of women and minorities selected as MacArthur Fellows because the award is given to very talented and accomplished individuals in the United States as citizens or permanent residents (green cardholders). This does not mean that gender and racial exclusion, which are prevalent in the American society, would not impact the number of qualified women and minorities who are selected for the Fellowship.

Chapter Two presents conceptual explanations or definitions of two interrelated words that are commonly used to refer or describe MacArthur Fellows: 'Genius and Creativity'. The public in the United States and the world and the national and international media refer to the Fellows as "Geniuses". The chapter explains the history behind this designation of Fellows as geniuses. It explains the impact such a designation has on the society as diverse as the United States and how it might impact women and minorities. As noted above, the MacArthur Fellows Program emphasizes that it has never and would not use the word genius to describe Fellows of the program. It instead said that it utilizes the word creative or creativity to describe selected Fellows. These two interrelated words or terms are at the core of the selection of individuals as Fellows. It is therefore useful to examine them.

Chapter Three presents the methodology of the study and any potential limitations. This chapter is important because it explains how the massive data in this study were collected or compiled, computed, and analyzed. Most readers would first want to read a methodology section of a study to determine the level of trust they would have of the data. This chapter examines over a dozen variables and presents explanations as to why the variables were selected for inclusion in this study. It also presents explanations or definitions of many of these variables, including gender, race, and educational attainment. For example, we will later learn that the racial categorization of people in the United States is very different from almost all countries in the world. It is therefore important to let readers know when a Fellow is categorized as Asian, Black, or White. The reason is that a White person in the United States is someone with ancestry from countries in Western or Southern Asia, Europe, and a child of parents, where one parent is Indian from India, Pakistan, Japan, Korea, or China, and a parent who is German, Irish or English.

Chapter Four presents the findings or results of this study. There are numerous interesting findings presented in this chapter. For example, women accounted for only 37% of all Fellows, while minorities accounted for almost 20 percent. Over half (51.3%) of the 1,014 Fellows are White men. Black men (7.2%), Asian men (3.94%), and Native American women (0.8%) have higher proportions than their adult proportions in the general population in 2018. Asians are the youngest Fellows, while Blacks are the oldest. Of the 1,014 Fellows, 78.3% were born in the United States. Of that total, 43.3% were born in the Northeast, with 173 of them born in New York state. Of the 220 Fellows born outside of the United States, 43.6% were born in Europe. The name John appeared the most among men and Susan appeared the most among women. Of the 965 terminal or highest degrees earned by 928 Fellows, 540 (56%) were doctorates, with the PhD accounting for 514 (53.3%). Harvard University awarded the highest number of degrees, 119, Yale University, 61; University of California, Berkeley, 51; Columbia University, 44; and Princeton University, 41. All eight Ivy League institutions awarded 306 (31.7%) degrees to 300 (32.3%) Fellows. The 2020 U.S. News and World Report Top 25 institutions combined awarded 522 (54.1%) degrees to 514 (55.5%) Fellows.

Chapter Five presents the discussion section of this study. In discussing the visible gender gap in this study, there appears to be a link among earned doctoral degrees, foreign-born males, and the overall gender gap in the study. The foreign-born data, with a very high male majority, tend to contribute to the selection of more men. This means that if the selection criteria for Fellows were limited to native-born United States citizens, then the gender gap could have been smaller. The reason is that females now account for the majority of associate, bachelor's, and master's degree holders. However, males continue to earn more professional and doctoral degrees, with foreign-born males responsible for this fact. Ivy League institutions continue to have a disproportionate representation in almost all top institutions within the American society, primarily because they are the oldest and wealthiest in the nation. The unusual racial categorization of people in the United States tends to hide or suppress the heritage of Fellows from Western Asia or Iran – because they are categorized as "White" by the Federal government, and the White racial category in the United States is equated with European. Immigration to the United States is responsible for Asians being the youngest Fellows. In the United States, both first and last names are powerful predictors of one's social and economic status in the society. Geographic location plays a crucial role in the selection of a Fellow at the time of award, whether it is the U.S. state, region, country, or continent where one resides. There is a serious competition for talented or skilled individuals amongst the states and regions in the United States, or amongst countries and continents in the world. Finally, Chapter Six presents the conclusion of the study. The chapter highlights the key findings in Chapter Four and their discussion in Chapter Five.

# CHAPTER TWO

## Defining Genius and Creativity

The public tends to refer to MacArthur Fellows as geniuses, while the MacArthur Fellows Program utilizes the word creative or creativity to refer to them or describe them. It has been widely noted that the MacArthur Fellows Program has never officially used the term genius to refer to Fellows. According to von Gunten (2009), "The popular press has generally characterized these as "genius" awards" (p.5). As Wooster (2014) notes: "The first article to refer to the fellowships as "genius grants" was written by Diane Shah in *Newsweek* in 1979—two years before the fellowship's program was started." According to the Managing Editor of the MacArthur Fellows Program, Dr Cecilia Conrad (2013): "The foundation does not use the name "genius" grant; the news media coined that nickname in 1981 when we announced our first class of fellows, and it stuck." Instead, the MacArthur Fellows Program has utilized the term creative or creativity. It is, therefore, useful to present definitions or explanations of both terms. A primary reason for this is that the definition of genius or creativity by one person may be different from another person's understanding of each term. As Goldberg (2017) points out, "… it's hard to tell who among the living truly is a genius" (p.C5). A careful examination of numerous scholarly journal articles, public intellectual journal articles, books, etc. shows various interrelated definitions of the terms genius and creativity, but debate exists as to what type of person should be considered a genius, or what the characteristics of a genius must be. Moreover, many of the definitions of the term genius include the term creativity, just as a number of the definitions of the term creativity includes the term genius. These definitions will help readers of this study to better understand how and why the over 1,000 MacArthur Fellows came to be selected in the almost four decades of the Program's existence. We will first start with the term genius and then the term creative or creativity.

## Definitions of a Genius

There are numerous definitions of the term genius. As Epstein (2013) points out: "The definitions for genius may be greater than the actual number of true geniuses" (p.38; also see Garber, 2002: 65). According to Kalb (2017): "Genius is too elusive, too subjective, too wedded to the verdict of history to be easily identified. And it requires the ultimate expression of too many traits to be simplified into the highest point on one human scale" (p.42). Brinkman (2010) notes that "The concept of genius is both revered and reviled in modern society" (p.124). Garber (2002) points out that: "The word "genius" derives from the same root as "gene" and "genetic," and meant originally, in Latin, a tutelary god or spirit given to every person at birth" (p.67). Garber (2002) adds that the term genius, which is an eighteenth-century word, "… continues to be, the Romantic hero, the loner, the eccentric, the apotheosis of the individual" (p.65). Andrews (2018) defines a genius as one with "exceptional intellectual or creative power or other natural ability" (p.27). Brinkman (2010) explains "… the components of creative genius, including talent, intelligence, memory, and the unconscious,…" (p.124; also see Benzon, 2018). Using the academic discipline or field of psychology to define genius using Intelligence Quotient (IQ) tests, Orner (2016) claims that the term describes "… a person who has an extraordinarily high level of intellectual power. … it is designated by exceptional creative ability and achievement" (also see Kalb, 2017: 42; Coutu, 2007: 122).

Epstein (2013) explains how rare geniuses are, and attempts to describe them by comparing them to learned individuals: "A man of learning is a man who has learned a great deal; a man of genius, one from whom we learn something which the genius has learned from nobody" (p.38). Epstein (2013) adds that: A genius is not merely brilliant, skillful, masterly, sometimes dazzling; he is miraculous, in the sense that his presence cannot be predicted, explained, or accounted for (at least thus far) by natural laws or scientific study" (p.38). Isaacson (2017) also compares a genius to a "supersmart" individual by pointing out that: "Smart people are a dime a dozen, and many of them don't amount to much. What matters is creativity, the ability to apply imagination to almost any situation" (p.62).

Patchett (2017) discusses who a genius is through the question of what it would require: "… knowing the thing you are meant to do in life and then doing it without regard for the time it will take?" (p.64). This means that hard work, dedication and perseverance are important components of being a genius. *As* von Gunten (2009) notes, "Thomas A. Edison is famously remembered to have said, 'Genius is 10% inspiration and 90% perspiration'" (p.5; also see Simonton, 2017: 126). According to Kalb (2017): "Natural gifts and a nurturing environment can still fall short of producing a genius, without motivation and tenacity propelling one forward. These personality traits, which pushed Darwin to spend two decades perfecting Origin of Species and Indian mathematician Srinivasa Ramanujan to produce thousands of formulas…" (p.47). Kalb (2017) cites a female MacArthur Fellow who notes that passion and perseverance combined, which she calls "grit" is the drive behind people's achievements. The idea of being a genius is not disguised within magic to make it seem that the important achievements of individuals happen spontaneously without hard work: "… there are differences when it comes to individual talent, but no matter how brilliant a person, fortitude, and discipline are critical to success. 'When you really look at somebody who accomplishes something great,'… it is not effortless'" (p.47). Kalb (2017) points out that one can attempt to understand the term genius: "… by unraveling the complex and tangled qualities—intelligence, creativity, perseverance, and simple good fortune, to name a few—that entwine to create a person capable of changing the world" (p.42).

One criticism of this concept of genius, which many tend to connect to those selected to become MacArthur Fellows, is that a higher percentage of individuals from certain groups or categories (sex/gender, race or ethnic origin), could be considered to be geniuses. For example, Kalb (2017) cites a scholar who cautioned people on the use of the word genius because it can "… be a societal judgment that elevates a chosen few while overlooking others—but to nurture imagination in everyone" (p.43). Goldberg (2017) also notes that the first time editors of the National Geographic magazine "… gathered portraits to create a gallery of geniuses past … the uniformity was obvious—and unsettling. In the sciences and arts, statecraft and literature, philosophy and industry, those hailed as geniuses were most often white men, of European origin" (p.C5).

The various definitions or explanations presented above as to who is a genius tend to show that it is someone who can either have formal or informal education. This person is passionate about a topic or multiple topics. He or she enjoys working for long hours on a task and is disciplined and persistent. He or she is so dedicated that they would persevere on a project even if it takes them decades to complete. To be a genius then is not just having mental skills, but also dedication and patience.

**Definitions of Creative or Creativity**

The term creative or creativity is regularly used by the MacArthur Fellows Program to describe its Fellows or potential future Fellows. The term creativity is also used widely in scholarly publications to describe talented or gifted individuals. On its website, the MacArthur Fellows Program states that its three criteria for the selection of Fellows are: (1) Exceptional creativity; (2) Promise for important future advances based on a track record of significant accomplishments; and (3) Potential for Fellowship to facilitate subsequent creative work ("About MacArthur Fellows Program," 2019). Many scholars and public intellectuals have presented interrelated definitions of the term creativity or creativist (Cox and Daniel, 1984; Starmer, 2013; Detlefsen, 2002; Kaufman and Sternberg, 2007; Lubart and Sternberg, 1998; Pieterse, 1996; Russ, 2016; Smirnov, 1994; Sternberg, 2003, 2006, 2012; Sternberg and Lubart, 1996; Torrance, 2004; Weisberg, 2010).

Sternberg and Lubart (1996) claim that "Creativity is the ability to produce work that is both novel (i.e. original or unexpected) and appropriate (i.e., useful or meets task constraints" (p.677). According to Kaufman and Sternberg (2007), explanations of creative ideas have three parts. The first part is that the ideas must be new, different, or be innovative: "Second, they need to be of high quality. Third, creative ideas must also be appropriate to the task at hand. Thus, a creative response to a problem is new, good, and relevant" (p.55). According to Sternberg (2006), creativity entails the convergence of six different but interrelated resources: "intellectual abilities, knowledge, styles of thinking, personality, motivation, and environment" (p.88).

Weisberg (2010) points out that "Creative thinking brings about new things" (p.235). Weisberg (2010) adds that in addition to creativity resulting in the creation of something new, "... an innovation is a new idea that is brought to the marketplace as a new product" (p.236). Weisberg (2010) also notes that: "Some argue that creativity is essentially a social activity because the attribution of creative to some product is done by others, based on its value" (p.237; also see Russ, 2016: 22 & 40).

Sternberg (2006) considers creativity to be a habit: "Behind all innovations one finds creativity, so innovations arise from a habit. When I speak of a habit, I refer to 'an acquired behavior pattern regularly followed until it has become almost involuntary'" (p.3; also see Torrance, 2004:6). According to Sternberg (2003):" Creativity is not an attribute limited to the historic 'greats'—the Darwins, the Picassos, the Hemingways. Rather, it is something anyone can use. To a large extent, creativity is a decision" (p.116). Pieterse (1998) describes a creativist view "… according to which people are the creative forces of development, the means as well as the end of development, for development is defined as people's self-development" (pp.352-353).

Simirnov (1994) describes what he calls creativists as individuals who search for common principle, and also tend to search: "… for its theoretical explanation. … Because of their interest in solving the theoretical problem, creativists will ignore the experimenter's instructions and stop or interrupt their own activity when necessary" (p.245). Lubart and Sternberg (1998) describe creative individuals in the world of ideas, as those who tend to buy low and sell high, and in doing so,they defy the masses in their creative big ideas. "Buying low means pursuing new or undervalued ideas that have growth potential-which may be successful for solving one's problem. Selling high means releasing a novel idea on the market when it has gained value and not holding an idea…" long enough that it becomes old (p.60).

According to Cox and Daniel (1984), MacArthur Fellows qualify for their awards because of their "… uncommon abilities, demonstrated across a broad spectrum of creative pursuits" (p.18). Russ (2016) reports on a study of MacArthur Fellows and college students on the topic of "pretend play" on their development. According to the findings, 26% of MacArthur Fellows and 12% of college students "… reported having imaginary worlds in childhood…. Other creative artists and scientists describe the importance of pretend play in their childhood and describe processes in their creativity that are similar to processes expressed in pretend play" (p.24; see Pieterse, 1998: 352-353).

According to Detlefsen (2002), in the late 19th and early 20th centuries, thinkers such as Hilber and Dedekind transferred the idea of freedom to an axiomatic setting. "These axiomatic creativists departed from the views of the earlier creativists by adding conditions that went beyond the traditional constraints of consistency and fruitfulness. One such constraint was a completeness condition, which Hilbert introduced as a kind of ideal or norm for creativist theorizing."

The explanations or definitions of both genius and creative or creativity tend to be very similar. Some explanations of creativity include the word genius and some definitions of genius include the word creative or creativity. This means that although the MacArthur Fellows Program claims that it does not use the word genius to describe its Fellows, it utilizes a word (creativity), which has the word in some of its definitions. It is important to note that although the findings in this study will show that the overwhelming majority of Fellows have earned terminal degrees, especially doctoral, Juris Doctorate, and Doctor of Medicine degrees, the public and media description of the Fellows as geniuses goes beyond college degree attainment because a significant proportion of Fellows did not attend or graduate from college. The creative or creativity definitions are also not limited to college degree attainment. This means that the Fellows can be described as highly skilled or talented individuals.

# CHAPTER THREE

## Methodology, Data Availability and Limitations of this Study

This research project started in June 2017. The data were collected from June 2017 to October 2018. It aims to make a useful contribution to the body of knowledge that has been produced on the MacArthur Fellows Program. The MacArthur Fellows Program presents the photos of almost all of its Fellows. It also presents background information of all Fellows under their names and photos, including profession, year fellowship was awarded, employment affiliation, geographic location when the fellowship was awarded, age at the time of award, and academic degrees (https://www.macfound.org/fellows/search/all). For Fellows without available photos on the MacArthur Fellows Program website, I searched their employment or personal websites or google image to find a photo of them.

The compilation of highly gifted individuals in almost four decades is a very important development because these individuals are from all walks of life and are recognized by both the MacArthur Foundation and the general public as creativists and geniuses. For example, the Fellows are professionals of all kinds: anthropologists, archaeologists, architects, artists, attorneys, authors, biologists, cartoonists, chemists, choreographers, civil rights leaders, community organizers, composers, computer scientists, conservationists, economists, educators, engineers, farmers, filmmakers, geologists, historians, illustrators, inventors, journalists, linguists, mathematicians, medical doctors, musicians, novelists, painters, paleobotanists, philosophers, physicists, planetary scientists, playwrights, poets, political scientists, psychologists, screenwriters and producers, sculptors, sociologists, statisticians, translators, and writers (Compiled by author based on data from https://www.macfound.org/fellows/search/all).

Most of the Fellows also work at great colleges and universities in the United States, including Arizona State University, Boston University, Brown University, Bryn Mawr, California Institute of Technology, Carnegie Mellon University, City University of New York, College of the Holy Cross, Columbia University, Drexel University, Harvard University,

Indiana University, Johns Hopkins University, Massachusetts Institute of Technology, Missouri State University, Northwestern University, New York University, Princeton University, Rockefeller University, Rutgers University, New Jersey, Stanford University, Stony Brook University, the University of California, Berkeley, University of California, Los Angeles, University of California, San Diego, the University of Chicago, University of Colorado, University of Illinois at Urbana-Champaign, University of Massachusetts, Amherst, University of Maryland, College Park, University of Michigan, University of New Hampshire, University of North Carolina, Chapel Hill, University of Tennessee, Knoxville, University of Texas, Austin, University of Pennsylvania, University of San Francisco, University of Southern California, University of Utah, University of Washington, University of Wisconsin, Milwaukee, Princeton University, State University of New York, Albany, Syracuse University, Vanderbilt University, Virginia Polytechnic Institute and State University, Wesleyan University, and Yale University.

However, while a significant body of research has examined various aspects of these Fellows, the public has not been provided with information showing the proportion of women and men, racial or ethnic backgrounds, or their highest or terminal degrees. This study aims to add these variables to the understanding of who these gifted individuals are.

The variables examined in this study include sex/gender, race/ethnicity, place of birth, age at the time of award, first name of Fellows, earned terminal/highest academic degree, type of academic degree, year academic degree is earned, alma mater, location of alma mater (U.S. state, region, and country), geographic location when fellowship is won (U.S. state or country), and year fellowship is won.

The sex/gender variable is based on a careful examination of the pictures of every Fellow and how they are described in the media or academic publications whether as he or she. There is one instance where the MacArthur Fellows Program did not identify a Fellow as he or she, and several media reports identified the individual as transsexual (from male to female). I, therefore, included that Fellow in the female/women category in this study.

The race variable is based on the classifications of the various racial groups by the United States federal government (Gans, 2012; Kaba, 2015, pp.120-121; "Standards for the Classification of Federal Data on Race and Ethnicity," 1995; Yancey 2003). For example, Kaba (2017a) cites the White House Office of Management and Budget as claiming that: "The term 'Black' in Directive No. 15 refers to a person having origins in any of the Black racial groups of Africa." Explaining who belongs to the White category: "In Directive No. 15, the 'White' category includes persons having origins in any of the original peoples of Europe, North Africa, or the Middle East" (p.20). This means that a Fellow with a visible or significant Black African blood is categorized as Black. A Fellow from South Asian nations such as Bangladesh, India, Pakistan or Sri Lanka, or East or Southeast Asian nations such as China, Japan, North Korea, South Korea, Philippines, Thailand, or Vietnam is categorized as Asian. A Fellow with ancestry from Israel, Turkey, Iran, Central Asia, or Arab is categorized as White. A Fellow with European ancestry is categorized as White. A Fellow with mixed Asian ancestry and any of the groups just categorized as White above is also categorized as White. There is one male Fellow with a Mexican mother and a Chinese father and he is categorized as Chinese (Asian) in this study. The reason is that most native Mexicans have DNA traced back to Asia.

The place or U.S. state and country of birth data were compiled and computed based on data posted on the website of the MacArthur Fellows Program. This is a very important information because it helps us to understand the ancestry of the Fellows. The reason is that a Fellow can be categorized as White, but it means that person can have heritage from Africa, Asia, and Europe. The place of birth data helps us to carefully examine some of the White Fellows and find out their ancestry. In fact, because of this information, the study identified a significant number of Fellows from Western Asia.

The educational attainment data focuses on a Fellow's earned highest or terminal college or higher education degrees. If a Fellow has an earned bachelor's degree or higher, I only count the highest degree. If he or she has any number of master's degrees only, I counted them all. If he or she has an earned master's and a JD, I counted only the JD. If he or she has an earned master's degree and a doctorate (such as PhD. or Ed.D.), I counted only the doctorate; I combined or counted a doctorate and an MD (Doctor of Medicine), or a doctorate and a JD (Juris Doctor). If a Fellow has one or more bachelor's degrees only, I counted them all. If a Fellow has one or more Associate degrees only (from a community or two-year college), I counted them all. If a Fellow has an MD and an MPA, MHA, or MBA, I only counted the MD. If a fellow has a JD and an L.L.M., I only counted the JD. The reason is that for the most part, one has to have a JD to qualify to get an L.L.M., but the vast majority of people with a JD do not seek an L.L.M. The types of academic degrees include B.A., B.S., M.A., M.S., Ph.D., and Ed.D. The MacArthur Fellows Program tends to periodically update the information of its Fellows, including educational attainment data. However, in the instances where I did not find a Fellow with a college degree on the MacArthur Fellows Program website, I searched the fellow's website and any relevant publications to determine whether he or she has an earned college degree. For example, it was through this method that I found out that the youngest female MacArthur Fellow, Lateefah Simon (who won the award at age 26 in 2003), in 2017, earned a bachelor's degree in public policy from Mills College in California.

The age at the time of award data were not available on the MacArthur Fellows website for three fellows (two men and one woman). However, I found such data for one male Fellow in a *New York Times* article about him after he was selected as a Fellow. For the remaining female and male Fellows, I utilized public information on their date of birth to determine their age at the time of the award.

The location of Fellows at the time of award data were not available for two male fellows on the website of the MacArthur Fellows Program. For one of these two Fellows, a newspaper discussed that fact as to how the MacArthur Fellows Program could not track his location at the time he won the award (Wooster, 2014). This information is useful because it helps to explain the intense competition among U.S. states and regions for talented individuals in the country. It is a sign of technological, economic, educational, and cultural prowess for a state to have a significant number or proportion of Fellows who work or reside in those states or regions when they were selected

The regional data are for both the four regions of the United States (Midwest, Northeast, South, and West) and the regions of the world based on the United Nations' categorization (see appendices section). I carefully rechecked all of the data I compiled several times for accuracy. For example, I added Taiwan under Eastern Asia, even though it is not listed in the United Nations regional classifications. There are two Fellows in this study born in Taiwan.

The first name variable is utilized in this study to follow-up on an April 24, 2018, *New York Times* study entitled, "The Top Jobs Where Women Are Outnumbered by Men Named John" focusing on the United States. The *New York Times* study also examined the first names of the 24 winners of the MacArthur Fellowship Awards in 2018 (Miller et al. 2018).

I did not contact any Fellow for any missing information about that Fellow. Apart from compiling the data from the MacArthur Fellows Program's website, I did not contact any official at the Program to request a particular information about a Fellow. As explained above, if the information is missing for a particular Fellow, I either clearly stateed that fact or I attempted to search the web for such information. The reason is that If I were to contact one person for missing information, they either would not feel comfortable providing such data or I may need to do the same for every Fellow with missing data. As a result, this study could not be completed.

I carefully rechecked all of the data I compiled several times for accuracy. For example, I was able to confirm the claim by the MacArthur Fellows Program that from 1981 to October 2018, 1,014. Fellows have been selected, through entering and counting the data of every single Fellow.

# CHAPTER FOUR

## Findings/Results and Analysis

### Gender/Sex and Racial Categories of MacArthur Fellows, 1981-2018

I have conducted numerous studies of prominent or gifted individuals in the past decade, and I have also examined studies conducted in the past several decades of such individuals. One finding that has remained constant in these studies is that regardless of race, ethnicity, or geographic location, males outnumber their female counterparts (Kaba, 2012b, 2013ab, 2015, 2016, 2017ab). This current study observes the continuation of that trend. For example, according to Table 1, of the 1,014 MacArthur Fellows selected from 1981 to 2018, 637 (62.8%) are men and 377 (37.2%) are women. Whites account for 815 (80.4%) of all Fellows. White men account for 520 (51.3%) of all Fellows, and 81.6% of all men. White women account for 295 (29.1%) of all Fellows, and 78.3% of all women. Blacks account for 127 (12.5%) of all Fellows. Black men account for 73 (7.2%) of all Fellows, and 11.5% of all men. Black women account for 54 (5.3%) of all Fellows, and 14.3% of all women. Asians account for 60 (5.9%) of all Fellows. Asian men account for 40 (3.9%) of all Fellows, and 6.3% of all men. Asian women account for 20 (1.98%) of all Fellows, and 5.3% of all women. Native Americans account for 12 (1.2%) of all Fellows. Native American women account for 8 (0.8%) of all Fellows, and 2.1% of all women. Native American men account for 4 (0.4%) of all Fellows, and 0.6% of all men (Table 1).

### Table 1. Sex/Gender and Racial Breakdowns of MacArthur Fellows, 1981 to 2018

| Race | Men | % of Men | % of Total | Women | % of Women | % of Total | Total | % of Total |
|---|---|---|---|---|---|---|---|---|
| Asian | 40 | 6.3 | 3.94 | 20 | 5.3 | 1.98 | 60 | 5.9 |
| Black | 73 | 11.5 | 7.2 | 54 | 14.3 | 5.3 | 127 | 12.5 |
| Native American | 4 | 0.6 | 0.4 | 8 | 2.1 | 0.8 | 12 | 1.2 |
| White | 520 | 81.6 | 51.3 | 295 | 78.3 | 29.1 | 815 | 80.4 |
| Total | 637 | 100 | 62.8 | 377 | 100 | 37.2 | 1014 | 100 |

Source: Compiled and computed based on data provided by the MacArthur Fellows Program (June 2017 to February 2019) at https://www.macfound.org/fellows/search/all.

## State/Country and Region of Birth of MacArthur Fellows, 1981 to 2018, by Sex and Race

The U.S. state and region, country, and world region where a Fellow is born is a piece of very important information. Geography is a very important variable, especially where one is born because they could have or lack any number of opportunities that would put them in a position to be selected as a MacArthur Fellow. Table 2 presents data on the place of birth of 1,013 (99.9%) of the 1,014 Fellows (data not available for one White male). Of the 1,013 Fellows, 793 (78.3%) were born in the United States or its territories and 220 (21.7%) were born outside of the United States.

Of the 793 Fellows born in the United States, 343 (43.3%) were born in the Northeast (including 173 in New York, 61 in Pennsylvania, 55 in Massachusetts, 27 in New Jersey, 17 in Connecticut, 6 in Rhode Island and 3 in Maine), but 33.9% of all Fellows; 182 (23%) Fellows were born in the South (including 32 in Washington, D.C., 22 in Texas, 21 in Maryland, 19 in Florida, 14 in Georgia, 12 in North Carolina, 9 in Alabama, 7 each in Louisiana and South Carolina, 6 each in Delaware, Kentucky, Mississippi, and Tennessee, 4 each in Arkansas, Oklahoma, and Virginia, and 3 in West Virginia), but 18% of all Fellows; 142 (18%) Fellows were born in the Midwest (including 44 in Illinois, 26 in Ohio, 24 in Michigan, 11 in Wisconsin, 9 in Minnesota, 8 each in Indiana and Missouri, 5 in Iowa, 4 in Nebraska, and 3 in Kansas), but 14% of all Fellows; 124 (15.6%) Fellows were born in the West (including 72 in California, 12 in Washington, 8 in Colorado, 6 in Idaho, 5 in New

Mexico, 3 each in Alaska, Arizona, Montana, Oregon and South Dakota, and 2 in Hawaii), but 12.2% of all Fellows; and 2 (0.25%, but 0.2% of all Fellows) Fellows were born in Puerto Rico.

Of the 220 Fellows born outside of the United States and its territories, 96 (43.6%) were born in Europe, but 9.5% of all Fellows; 53 (24.1%) Fellows were born in Asia, but 5.2% of all Fellows; 33 (15%) were born in Latin America and the Caribbean, but 3.3% of all Fellows; 14 (6.4%) Fellows were born in Africa, but 1.4% of all Fellows; and 8 (3.6%) Fellows were born in Oceania, but 0.8% of all Fellows.

Of the 96 Fellows born in Europe, 34 (35.4%) were born in Northern Europe (including 25 in the United Kingdom, and 2 each in Denmark, Ireland, and Latvia), but 3.4% of all Fellows; 32 (33.3%) Fellows were born in Western Europe (including 14 in Germany, 9 in France, 4 in Austria, and 2 each in the Netherlands and Switzerland), but 3.2% of all Fellows; 21 (21.8%) Fellows were born in Eastern Europe (including 8 in Russia, 4 in Romania, 3 in Poland, and 2 each in Czechoslovakia and Ukraine), but 2.1% of all Fellows; and 9 (9.4%) Fellows were born in Southern Europe (including 2 each in Greece, Italy, and Spain), but 0.9% of all Fellows.

Of the 53 Fellows born in Asia, 24 (45.2%) were born in Eastern Asia (including 17 in China, 4 in Japan, and 2 in Taiwan), but 2.4% of all Fellows; 13 (24.5%) Fellows were born in Southern Asia (10 in India and 3 in Pakistan), but 1.3% of all Fellows; 10 (18.9%) Fellows were born in Western Asia (including 5 in Israel and 2 in Lebanon), but 0.99% of all Fellows; and 6 (11.3%) Fellows were born in South-eastern Asia (including 4 in Vietnam), but 0.6% of all Fellows. Of the 33 Fellows born in Latin America and the Caribbean, 16 (48.5%) were born in South America (including 5 in Argentina, 3 each in Brazil and Chile, and 2 in Ecuador), but 1.6% of all Fellows; 11 (33.3%) Fellows were born in the Caribbean (including 5 in Cuba); and 5 (18.3%) Fellows were born in Central America (all 5 in Mexico), but 0.6% of all Fellows. Of the 14 (6.4%) Fellows born in Africa, 5 (35.7%) each were born in Northern Africa (Egypt, Libya, Morocco, Tunisia, and Sudan) and Western Africa (3 in Nigeria and 1 each in Ghana and Liberia), but 0.5% of all Fellows; and 4 (28.6%) Fellows were born in Eastern Africa (3 in Ethiopia and 1 in Kenya), but 0.4% of all Fellows. Of the 8 Fellows born in Oceania, 7 (87.5%) were born in Australia; and 1 (12.5%, but 0.8% of all Fellows) Fellow was born in New Zealand.

Racially, of the 814 White Fellows, 652 (80.1%) were born in the United States and its territories (405 men and 247 women). Of the 652 White Fellows born in the United States and its territories, 305 (46.8%) were born in the Northeast (199 men, including 108 in New York; and 106 women, including 43 in New York); 129 (19.8%) were born in the South (74 men, including 19 in Washington, D.C.; and 55 women, including 9 each in Washington D.C. and Texas); 114 (17.5%) were born in the Midwest (70 men, including 22 in Illinois; and 44 women, including 15 in Illinois); and 103 (15.8%) were born in the West (61 men, including 40 in California; and 42 women, including 24 in California).

All 16 Fellows born in Canada are White (10 men and 6 women). Of the 14 Fellows born in Africa, 4 (28.6%) Whites are born in four countries in Northern Africa (3 women, born in Egypt, Morocco, and Tunisia; and 1 man born in Libya). The 4 White Fellows born in Africa account for 0.5% of the 814 Whites. Of the 53 Fellows born in Asia, 12 (22.6%) are White (8 men and 4 women). Of the 12 White Fellows born in Asia, 10 (83.3%) were born in Western Asia (7 men, including 3 in Israel, 2 in Lebanon, and 1 each in Jordan and Turkey; and 3 women, including 2 in Israel and 1 in Syria) and 2 were born in Eastern Asia (1 man in China and 1 woman in Taiwan). The 12 Whites born in Asia account for 1.5% of all 814 Whites.

Of the 33 Fellows born in Latin America and the Caribbean, 27 (81.8%) are White (18 men and 9 women). Of the 27 White Fellows born in Latin America and the Caribbean, 16 (59.3%) were born in South America (11 men, including 3 each born in Argentina and Chile, and 2 in Brazil; and 5 women, including 2 born in Argentina, and 1 each in Brazil, Colombia, and Ecuador); 6 (22.2%) were born in Central America (4 men, including 3 in Mexico and 1 in Guatemala; and 2 women, both born in Mexico); and 5 (18.5%) born in the Caribbean (3 men, all born in Cuba; and 2 women, 1 each in the Bahamas and Cuba). The 27 Whites born in Latin America and the Caribbean account for 3.3% of all 814 Whites.

All 96 (11.8% of 814 Whites) Fellows born in Europe are White (72 men and 24 women). Of the 96 White Fellows born in Europe, 34 (35.4%) were born in Northern Europe (26 men, including 21 born in the United Kingdom; and 8 women, including 4 born in the United Kingdom and 2 in Latvia); 32 (33.3%) were born in Western Europe (21 men, including 9 in Germany, 6 in France, 3 in Austria, and 2 in the Netherlands; and 11 women, including 5 in Germany and 3 in France); 21 (21.9%) were born in Eastern Europe (17 men, including 7 in Russia,

3 in Romania, and 2 each in Czechoslovakia, Poland, Ukraine; and 4 women, 1 each in Moldova, Poland, Romania, and Russia); and 9 (9.4%) were born in Southern Europe (8 men, including 2 each in Italy and Spain; and 1 woman born in Greece).

Of the 8 Fellows born in Oceania, 7 (87.5%) are White. Of the 7 White Fellows born in Oceania, 6 (87.5%) were born in Australia (4 men and 2 women) and 1 (14.3%) man was born in New Zealand. The 7 Whites born in Oceania account for 0.9% of all 814 Whites.

Of the 127 Black Fellows, 112 (88.1%) were born in the United States and its territories (66 men and 46 women). Of the 112 Black Fellows born in the United States, 51 (45.5%) were born in the South (29 men, including 4 each in Washington, D.C. and Florida; and 22 women, including 5 in Alabama and 4 in Maryland); 28 (25%) were born in the Northeast (18 men, including 12 in New York; and 8 women, including 5 in New York); 24 (21.4%) were born in the Midwest (14 men, including 6 in Illinois; and 10 women, including 5 in Ohio); and 8 (7.1%) were born in the West (4 men, including 2 in California; and 4 women, including 3 in California).

Of the 15 (11.8% of 127 total) Blacks born outside of the United States and its territories, 9 (60%) were born in Africa (6 women and 3 men), and 6 (40%) in the Caribbean. Of the 9 Blacks born in Africa, 5 (55.6%) were born in Western Africa (4 women, 3 in Nigeria and 1 in Liberia; and 1 man born in Ghana); 3 (33.3%) in Eastern Africa (Ethiopia, including 2 men and 1 woman); and 1 was born in Northern Africa (a woman born in Sudan). Of the 6 Blacks born in the Caribbean, 4 are men (1 each born in Cuba, the Dominican Republic, Saint Lucia, and Trinidad and Tobago) and 2 are women (born in Haiti and Jamaica).

Of the 60 Asian Fellows, 17 (28.3%) were born in the United States and its territories (11 men and 6 women). Of the 17 Asian Fellows born in the United States, 9 (52.9%) were born in the Northeast (6 men, including 5 in New York; and 3 women, including 2 in Pennsylvania); 4 were born in the West (2 men, born in Arizona and California; and 2 women, born in California and Hawaii); 2 each in the Midwest (one man and one woman born in Wisconsin) and the South (both men, born in Alabama and Maryland).

Of the 43 (71.7% of all 60 total) Asians born outside of the United States and its territories, 41 (95.3%) were born in Asia (27 men and 14 women) and 1 each was born in Africa (a man born in Kenya, East

Africa) and Oceania (a man born in Australia). Of the 41 Asians born in Asia, 22 (53.7%) were born in Eastern Asia (13 men, including 10 in China, and 1 each in Japan, South Korea, and Taiwan; and 9 women, including 6 born in China and 3 in Japan); 13 (31.7%) were born in Southern Asia (10 men, all born in India; and 3 women, all born in Pakistan); and 6 (14.6%) were born in South-eastern Asia (4 men, including 2 born in Vietnam, and 1 each born in Cambodia and the Philippines; and 2 women, both born in Vietnam) (Table 2).

All 12 Native American Fellows were born in the United States: 9 (75%) in the West (7 women in 7 different states: Alaska, Arizona, California, Idaho, Montana, New Mexico, and Washington; and 2 men born in Alaska and New Mexico); 2 (16.7%) were born in the Midwest (2 men born in Ohio and Nebraska); and 1 (8.3%) woman was born in the Northeast (Massachusetts).

Table 2. State/Country and Region of Birth of MacArthur Fellows, 1981 to 2018, by Sex and Race

| Northeast | # | White | % | Men | Women | Black | % | Men | Women | Asian | % | Men | Women | Native American | % | Men | Women |
|---|---|---|---|---|---|---|---|---|---|---|---|---|---|---|---|---|---|
| New York | 173 | 151 | 87.3 | 108 | 43 | 17 | 9.8 | 12 | 5 | 5 | 3 | 5 | | | | | |
| Pennsylvania | 61 | 52 | 85.2 | 34 | 18 | 7 | 11.7 | 5 | 2 | 2 | 3 | | 2 | | | | |
| Massachusetts | 55 | 51 | 92.7 | 26 | 25 | 2 | 3.6 | | 2 | 2 | 1 | 1.8 | 1 | | 1 | 1.8 | | 1 |
| New Jersey | 27 | 25 | 92.6 | 16 | 9 | 2 | 7.4 | 1 | 1 | | | | | | | | |
| Connecticut | 17 | 16 | 94 | 7 | 9 | | | | | 1 | 5.9 | | 1 | | | | |
| Rhode Island | 6 | 6 | 100 | 5 | 1 | | | | | | | | | | | | |
| Maine | 3 | 3 | 100 | 2 | 1 | | | | | | | | | | | | |
| New Hampshire | 1 | 1 | 100 | 1 | | | | | | | | | | | | | |
| Total | 343 | 305 | 88.9 | 199 | 106 | 28 | 8.2 | 18 | 10 | 9 | 2.6 | 6 | 3 | 1 | 0.3 | | 1 |
| % of U.S. total | 43.3 | 38.5 | | 25 | 13 | 3.5 | | 2.3 | 1.3 | 1.1 | | 0.8 | 0.4 | 0.1 | | | 0.1 |
| % of all Fellows | 33.9 | 30.1 | | 19.6 | 10.5 | 2.8 | | 1.8 | 1.0 | 0.9 | | 0.6 | 0.3 | 0.099 | | | 0.099 |
| | | | | | | | | | | | | | | | | | |
| Midwest | | | | | | | | | | | | | | | | | |
| Illinois | 44 | 37 | 84.1 | 22 | 15 | 7 | 15.9 | 6 | 1 | | | | | | | | |
| Ohio | 26 | 18 | 69.2 | 10 | 8 | 7 | 26.9 | 2 | 5 | | | | | 1 | 3.8 | 1 | |
| Michigan | 24 | 20 | 83.3 | 14 | 6 | 4 | 16.7 | 1 | 3 | | | | | | | | |

| | | | | | | | | | | | | | | | | | |
|---|---|---|---|---|---|---|---|---|---|---|---|---|---|---|---|---|---|
| Wisconsin | 11 | 9 | 81.8 | 6 | 3 | | | | | 2 | 18.2 | 1 | 1 | | | | |
| Minnesota | 9 | 8 | 88.9 | 4 | 4 | 1 | 11.1 | 1 | | | | | | | | | |
| Indiana | 8 | 7 | 87.5 | 5 | 2 | 1 | 12.5 | 1 | | | | | | | | | |
| Missouri | 8 | 6 | 75 | 3 | 3 | 2 | 25 | 2 | | | | | | | | | |
| Iowa | 5 | 4 | 80 | 3 | 1 | 1 | 20 | | 1 | | | | | | | | |
| Nebraska | 4 | 3 | 75 | 1 | 2 | | | | | | | | | 1 | 25 | 1 | |
| Kansas | 3 | 2 | 66.7 | 2 | | 1 | | 1 | | | | | | | | | |
| Total | 142 | 114 | 80.3 | 70 | 44 | 24 | 16.9 | 14 | 10 | 2 | 1.4 | 1 | 1 | 2 | 1.4 | 2 | |
| % of U.S. total | 18.0 | 14.4 | | 8.8 | 5.5 | 3.0 | | 1.8 | 1.3 | 0.3 | | 0.1 | 0.1 | 0.3 | | 0.3 | |
| % of all Fellows | 14.0 | 11.3 | | 6.9 | 4.3 | 2.4 | | 1.4 | 0.99 | 0.2 | | 0.099 | 0.099 | 0.2 | | 0.2 | |
| | | | | | | | | | | | | | | | | | |
| South | | | | | | | | | | | | | | | | | |
| Washington, D.C. | 32 | 28 | 87.5 | 19 | 9 | 4 | 12.5 | 4 | | | | | | | | | |
| Texas | 22 | 18 | 81.8 | 9 | 9 | 4 | 18.2 | 2 | 2 | | | | | | | | |
| Maryland | 21 | 14 | 66.7 | 6 | 8 | 6 | 28.6 | 2 | 4 | 1 | 5 | 1 | | | | | |
| Florida | 19 | 14 | 73.7 | 7 | 7 | 5 | 26.3 | 4 | 1 | | | | | | | | |
| Georgia | 14 | 10 | 71.4 | 7 | 3 | 4 | 28.6 | 1 | 3 | | | | | | | | |
| North Carolina | 12 | 10 | 83.3 | 6 | 4 | 2 | 16.7 | 1 | 1 | | | | | | | | |
| Alabama | 9 | 1 | 11.1 | | 1 | 7 | 77.8 | 2 | 5 | 1 | 11 | 1 | | | | | |
| Louisiana | 7 | 4 | 57.1 | 1 | 3 | 3 | 42.9 | 2 | 1 | | | | | | | | |
| South Carolina | 7 | 3 | 42.9 | 2 | 1 | 4 | 57.1 | 1 | 3 | | | | | | | | |
| Delaware | 6 | 5 | 83.3 | 2 | 3 | 1 | 16.7 | 1 | | | | | | | | | |
| Kentucky | 6 | 5 | 83.3 | 3 | 2 | 1 | 16.7 | | 1 | | | | | | | | |
| Mississippi | 6 | 3 | 50 | 2 | 1 | 3 | 50 | 3 | | | | | | | | | |
| Tennessee | 6 | 3 | 50 | 2 | 1 | 3 | 50 | 2 | 1 | | | | | | | | |
| Arkansas | 4 | 2 | 50 | 1 | 1 | 2 | 50 | 2 | | | | | | | | | |
| Oklahoma | 4 | 4 | 100 | 3 | 1 | | | | | | | | | | | | |
| Virginia | 4 | 3 | 75 | 2 | 1 | 1 | | 1 | | | | | | | | | |
| West Virginia | 3 | 2 | 66.7 | 2 | | 1 | | 1 | | | | | | | | | |
| Total | 182 | 129 | 70.9 | 74 | 55 | 51 | 28 | 29 | 22 | 2 | 1.1 | 2 | | | | | |
| % of U.S. total | 23.0 | 16.3 | | 9.3 | 6.9 | 6.4 | | 3.7 | 2.8 | 0.3 | | 0.3 | | | | | |

| | | | | | | | | | | | | | | | | |
|---|---|---|---|---|---|---|---|---|---|---|---|---|---|---|---|---|
| % of all Fellows | 18 | 12.7 | | 7 | 5.4 | 5 | 2.8 | 2.9 | 2.2 | 0.2 | | 0.2 | | | | |
| | | | | | | | | | | | | | | | | |
| West | | | | | | | | | | | | | | | | |
| California | 72 | 64 | 88.9 | 40 | 24 | 5 | 6.9 | 2 | 3 | 2 | 3 | 1 | 1 | 1 | 1 | 1 |
| Washington | 12 | 11 | 91.7 | 6 | 5 | | | | | | | 1 | 8.3 | | | 1 |
| Colorado | 8 | 7 | 87.5 | 2 | 5 | 1 | 12.5 | 1 | | | | | | | | |
| Idaho | 6 | 5 | 83.3 | 1 | 4 | | | | | | | 1 | 16.7 | | | 1 |
| New Mexico | 5 | 2 | 40 | 2 | | 1 | 20 | 1 | | | | 2 | 40 | 1 | | 1 |
| Alaska | 3 | 1 | 33.3 | 1 | | | | | | | | 2 | 66.7 | 1 | | 1 |
| Arizona | 3 | 1 | 33.3 | 1 | | | | | 1 | 33.3 | 1 | 1 | 33.3 | | | 1 |
| Montana | 3 | 2 | 66.7 | 2 | | | | | | | | 1 | 33.3 | | | 1 |
| Oregon | 3 | 2 | 66.7 | 1 | 1 | 1 | 33.3 | | 1 | | | | | | | |
| South Dakota | 3 | 3 | 100 | 3 | | | | | | | | | | | | |
| Hawaii | 2 | 1 | 50 | 1 | | | | | 1 | 50 | 1 | | | | | |
| North Dakota | 2 | 2 | 100 | | 2 | | | | | | | | | | | |
| Utah | 2 | 2 | 100 | 1 | 1 | | | | | | | | | | | |
| Total | 124 | 103 | 83.1 | 61 | 42 | 8 | 6.5 | 4 | 4 | 4 | 3.2 | 2 | 2 | 9 | 7.3 | 2 | 7 |
| % of U.S. Total | 15.6 | 13.0 | | 7.7 | 5.3 | 1.0 | | 0.5 | 0.5 | 0.5 | | 0.3 | 0.3 | 1.1 | | 0.3 | 0.9 |
| % of all Fellows | 12.2 | 10.3 | | 6 | 4.1 | 0.8 | | 0.4 | 0.4 | 0.4 | | 0.2 | 0.2 | 0.9 | | 0.2 | 0.7 |
| | | | | | | | | | | | | | | | | |
| Caribbean United States | | | | | | | | | | | | | | | | |
| Puerto Rico | 2 | 1 | 50 | 1 | 50 | 1 | 50 | 1 | | | | | | | | |
| United States Total | 793 | 652 | 82.2 | 405 | 247 | 112 | 14.1 | 66 | 46 | 17 | 2.1 | 11 | 6 | 12 | 1.5 | 4 | 8 |
| % of all Fellows | 78.3 | 64.4 | | 40 | 24.4 | 11.1 | | 6.5 | 4.5 | 1.7 | | 1.1 | 0.6 | 1.2 | | 0.4 | 0.8 |
| | | | | | | | | | | | | | | | | |
| Canada | 16 | 16 | 100 | 10 | 6 | | | | | | | | | | | | |
| % of all Fellows | 1.6 | 1.6 | | 0.99 | 0.6 | | | | | | | | | | | | |
| | | | | | | | | | | | | | | | | |
| Northern America | 809 | 668 | 82.6 | 415 | 253 | 112 | 13.8 | 66 | 46 | 17 | 2.1 | 11 | 6 | 12 | 1.48 | 4 | 8 |
| % of all Fellows | 80 | 65.9 | | 41 | 25 | 11.1 | | 6.5 | 4.5 | 1.7 | | 1.1 | 0.6 | 1.2 | | 0.4 | 0.8 |
| | | | | | | | | | | | | | | | | |
| Africa | | | | | | | | | | | | | | | | |

| | | | | | | | | | | | | | | |
|---|---|---|---|---|---|---|---|---|---|---|---|---|---|---|
| Eastern Africa | | | | | | | | | | | | | | |
| Ethiopia | 3 | | | | 3 | 100 | 2 | 1 | | | | | | |
| Kenya | 1 | | | | | | | | 1 | 100 | 1 | | | |
| Total | 4 | | | | 3 | 75 | 2 | 1 | 1 | 25 | 1 | | | |
| % of all Fellows | 0.4 | | | | 0.3 | | 0.2 | 0.099 | 0.099 | | 0.099 | | | |
| | | | | | | | | | | | | | | |
| Northern Africa | | | | | | | | | | | | | | |
| Egypt | 1 | 1 | 100 | | 1 | | | | | | | | | |
| Libya | 1 | 1 | 100 | 1 | | | | | | | | | | |
| Morocco | 1 | 1 | 100 | | 1 | | | | | | | | | |
| Tunisia | 1 | 1 | 100 | | 1 | | | | | | | | | |
| Sudan | 1 | | | | 1 | 100 | | 1 | | | | | | |
| Total | 5 | 4 | 80 | 1 | 3 | 1 | 20 | | 1 | | | | | |
| % of all Fellows | 0.5 | 0.4 | | 0.099 | 0.3 | 0.099 | | | 0.099 | | | | | |
| | | | | | | | | | | | | | | |
| Western Africa | | | | | | | | | | | | | | |
| Ghana | 1 | | | | 1 | 100 | 1 | | | | | | | |
| Liberia | 1 | | | | 1 | 100 | | 1 | | | | | | |
| Nigeria | 3 | | | | 3 | 100 | | 3 | | | | | | |
| Total | 5 | | | | 5 | 100 | 1 | 4 | | | | | | |
| % of all Fellows | | | | | | | | | | | | | | |
| Africa Total | 14 | 4 | 28.6 | 1 | 3 | 9 | 64.3 | 3 | 6 | 1 | 7.1 | 1 | | |
| % of all Fellows | 1.4 | 0.4 | | 0.099 | 0.3 | 0.9 | | 0.3 | 0.6 | 0.099 | | 0.099 | | |
| | | | | | | | | | | | | | | |
| Asia | | | | | | | | | | | | | | |
| Eastern Asia | | | | | | | | | | | | | | |
| China | 17 | 1 | 5.9 | 1 | | | | | | 16 | 94.1 | 10 | 6 | |
| Japan | 4 | | | | | | | | | 4 | 100 | 1 | 3 | |
| South Korea | 1 | | | | | | | | | 1 | 100 | 1 | | |
| Taiwan | 2 | 1 | 50 | | 1 | | | | | 1 | 50 | 1 | | |
| Total | 24 | 2 | 83.3 | 1 | 1 | | | | | 22 | 91.7 | 13 | 9 | |

| | | | | | | | | | | | | | |
|---|---|---|---|---|---|---|---|---|---|---|---|---|---|
| % of all Fellows | 2.4 | 0.2 | | 0.1 | 0.1 | | | 2.2 | 9.1 | 1.3 | 0.9 | | |
| | | | | | | | | | | | | | |
| South-eastern Asia | | | | | | | | | | | | | |
| Cambodia | 1 | | | | | | | 1 | 100 | 1 | | | |
| Philippines | 1 | | | | | | | 1 | 100 | 1 | | | |
| Vietnam | 4 | | | | | | | 4 | 100 | 2 | 2 | | |
| Total | 6 | | | | | | | 6 | 100 | 4 | 2 | | |
| % of all Fellows | 0.6 | | | | | | | 0.6 | | 0.4 | 0.2 | | |
| | | | | | | | | | | | | | |
| Southern Asia | | | | | | | | | | | | | |
| India | 10 | | | | | | | 10 | 100 | 10 | | | |
| Pakistan | 3 | | | | | | | 3 | 100 | | 3 | | |
| Total | 13 | | | | | | | 13 | 100 | 10 | 3 | | |
| % of all Fellows | 1.3 | | | | | | | 1.3 | | 0.99 | 0.3 | | |
| | | | | | | | | | | | | | |
| Western Asia | | | | | | | | | | | | | |
| Isreal | 5 | 5 | 100 | 3 | 2 | | | | | | | | |
| Jordan | 1 | 1 | 100 | 1 | | | | | | | | | |
| Lebanon | 2 | 2 | 100 | 2 | | | | | | | | | |
| Syria | 1 | 1 | 100 | | 1 | | | | | | | | |
| Turkey | 1 | 1 | 100 | 1 | | | | | | | | | |
| Total | 10 | 10 | 100 | 7 | 3 | | | | | | | | |
| % of all Fellows | 0.99 | 0.99 | | 0.7 | 0.3 | | | | | | | | |
| Asia Total | 53 | 12 | 22.6 | 8 | 4 | | | 41 | 77.4 | 27 | 14 | | |
| % of all Fellows | 5.2 | 1.2 | | 0.8 | 0.4 | | | 4.1 | 7.6 | 2.7 | 1.4 | | |
| | | | | | | | | | | | | | |
| Caribbean | | | | | | | | | | | | | |
| Bahamas | 1 | 1 | 100 | | 1 | | | | | | | | |
| Cuba | 5 | 4 | 80 | 3 | 1 | 1 | 100 | 1 | | | | | |
| Dominican Republic | 1 | | | | | 1 | 100 | 1 | | | | | |
| Haiti | 1 | | | | | 1 | 100 | | 1 | | | | |
| Jamaica | 1 | | | | | 1 | 100 | | 1 | | | | |

| | | | | | | | | | |
|---|---|---|---|---|---|---|---|---|---|
| Saint Lucia | 1 | | | | 1 | 100 | 1 | | |
| Trinidad and Tobago | 1 | | | | 1 | 100 | 1 | | |
| Total | 11 | 5 | 45.5 | 3 | 2 | 6 | 54.5 | 4 | 2 |
| % of all Fellows | 1.1 | 0.5 | | 0.3 | 0.2 | 0.6 | | 0.4 | 0.2 |
| | | | | | | | | | |
| Latin America | | | | | | | | | |
| Central America | | | | | | | | | |
| Guatemala | 1 | 1 | 100 | 1 | | | | | |
| Mexico | 5 | 5 | 100 | 3 | 2 | | | | |
| Total | 6 | 6 | 100 | 4 | 2 | | | | |
| % of all Fellows | 0.6 | 0.6 | | 0.4 | 0.2 | | | | |
| | | | | | | | | | |
| South America | | | | | | | | | |
| Argentina | 5 | 5 | 100 | 3 | 2 | | | | |
| Brazil | 3 | 3 | 100 | 2 | 1 | | | | |
| Chile | 3 | 3 | 100 | 3 | | | | | |
| Colombia | 1 | 1 | 100 | | 1 | | | | |
| Ecuador | 2 | 2 | 100 | 1 | 1 | | | | |
| Paraguay | 1 | 1 | 100 | 1 | | | | | |
| Venezuela | 1 | 1 | 100 | 1 | | | | | |
| Total | 16 | 16 | 100 | 11 | 5 | | | | |
| % of all Fellows | 1.6 | 1.6 | | 1 | | | | | |
| Latin Ame. & Caribbean | 33 | 27 | 81.8 | 18 | 9 | 6 | 18.2 | 4 | 2 |
| % of all Fellows | 3.3 | 2.7 | | 2 | 0.9 | 0.6 | | 0.4 | 0.2 |
| | | | | | | | | | |
| Europe | | | | | | | | | |
| Eastern Europe | | | | | | | | | |
| Czechoslovakia | 2 | 2 | 100 | 2 | | | | | |
| Hungary | 1 | 1 | 100 | 1 | | | | | |
| Moldova | 1 | 1 | 100 | | 1 | | | | |

| | | | | | |
|---|---|---|---|---|---|
| Poland | 3 | 3 | 100 | 2 | 1 |
| Romania | 4 | 4 | 100 | 3 | 1 |
| Russia | 8 | 8 | 100 | 7 | 1 |
| Ukraine | 2 | 2 | 100 | 2 | |
| Total | 21 | 21 | 100 | 17 | 4 |
| % of all Fellows | 2.1 | 2.1 | | 2 | 0 |
| | | | | | |
| Northern Europe | | | | | |
| Denmark | 2 | 2 | 100 | 1 | 1 |
| Estonia | 1 | 1 | 100 | 1 | |
| Ireland | 2 | 2 | 100 | 1 | 1 |
| Latvia | 2 | 2 | 100 | | 2 |
| Lithuania | 1 | 1 | 100 | 1 | |
| Sweden | 1 | 1 | 100 | 1 | |
| United Kingdom | 25 | 25 | 100 | 21 | 4 |
| Total | 34 | 34 | | 26 | 8 |
| % of all Fellows | 3.4 | 3.4 | | 3 | 0.8 |
| | | | | | |
| Southern Europe | | | | | |
| Bosnia | 1 | 1 | 100 | 1 | |
| Croatia | 1 | 1 | 100 | 1 | |
| Greece | 2 | 2 | 100 | 1 | 1 |
| Italy | 2 | 2 | 100 | 2 | |
| Spain | 2 | 2 | 100 | 2 | |
| Yugoslavia | 1 | 1 | 100 | 1 | |
| Total | 9 | 9 | 100 | 8 | 1 |
| % of all Fellows | 0.9 | 0.9 | | 1 | 0.099 |
| | | | | | |
| Western Europe | | | | | |
| Austria | 4 | 4 | 100 | 3 | 1 |
| Belgium | 1 | 1 | 100 | | 1 |
| France | 9 | 9 | 100 | 6 | 3 |

| | | | | | | | | | | | | | | | |
|---|---|---|---|---|---|---|---|---|---|---|---|---|---|---|---|
| Germany | 14 | 14 | 100 | 9 | 5 | | | | | | | | | | |
| Netherlands | 2 | 2 | 100 | 2 | | | | | | | | | | | |
| Switzerland | 2 | 2 | 100 | 1 | 1 | | | | | | | | | | |
| Total | 32 | 32 | 100 | 21 | 11 | | | | | | | | | | |
| % of all Fellows | 3.2 | 3.2 | | 2.1 | 1.1 | | | | | | | | | | |
| Europe Total | 96 | 96 | 100 | 72 | 24 | | | | | | | | | | |
| % of all Fellows | 9.5 | 9.5 | | 7.1 | 2.4 | | | | | | | | | | |
| Oceania | | | | | | | | | | | | | | | |
| | | | | | | | | | | | | | | | |
| | | | | | | | | | | | | | | | |
| % of all Fellows | 0.8 | 0.7 | | 0.5 | 0.2 | | | | 0.099 | | 0.099 | | | | |
| All Fellows | 1013 | 814 | 80.4 | 519 | 295 | 127 | 12.5 | 73 | 54 | 60 | 5.9 | 40 | 20 | 12 | 1.2 | 4 | 8 |

Source: Compiled and computed based on data provided by the MacArthur Fellows Program (June 2017 to February 2019) at https://www.macfound.org/fellows/search/all.

## First Names of MacArthur Fellows, 1981 to 2018

Most research on names tend to focus on last or surnames and first names. Some of the reasons for this may include marriage, where in most cases wives tend to take the last names or surnames of their husbands. In the United States, assimilation has been a reason individuals would change their first name or surname and take on more 'mainstream' or northern or Western European names. Recent scholarship on first or surnames tend to focus on 'social taste', sports, cultural heritage or origins, crime, publications of peer-reviewed scholarly journal articles, citations and indexing of authors of scholarly publications, and salary of school principals (Abramo and D'Angelo, 2017; Alexander and Ward, 2018; Besnard and Desplanques, 2001; Carneiro et al., 2020; Comenetz, 2016; Kalist and Lee, 2005; Lasker, 1991; Lieberson and Bell, 1992; Lv and Newman Young, 2014; Raveenthiran, 2016; Tzioumis, 2018;

Williams, 2005; Voracek et al., 2015; Wuffle and Coulter, 2014; Young and Castaneda, 2008).

For this current study, among women, Table 3a shows that the only female first name in double figures among all 377 female Fellows is Susan, with 11 (2.9%), with all of them being White. There is also one Fellow each with a similar name: Sue, Suzanne, and Suzan-Lori. Other names that appear 3 times or more are: Nancy and Sarah, 7 (1.9%) each, all White (the name Sara also appeared 3 times, with 2 Whites and 1 Black); Deborah, 6 (1.6%), including 4 Whites, 1 Black and 1 Asian; Julie, 6 (1.6%), including 4 Whites, 1 Black and 1 Asian; Patricia, 6 (1.6%), 4 Whites, 1 Black, and 1 Native American; Rebecca, 6 (1.6%), all White; Claire, Elizabeth, and Margaret, 5 (1.3%) each, (all White); Jennifer, 5 (1.3%), including 3 Whites and 2 Blacks; Mary, 5, (1.3%), including 4 Whites and 1 Black; Amy, Ann, Heather, Maria, and Ruth, each 4 (1.1%), all White (the name Anne also appeared 2 times); Anna and Ellen, 4 (1.1%), each including 3 Whites and 1 Black; Lisa, 4 (1.1%), 2 Whites and 2 Blacks; Angela, 3 (0.8%), including 1 White, 1 Black and 1 Asian; Barbara, 3 (0.8%), 2 Whites and 1 Black; Carolyn, 3 (0.8%), all White; Janine, 3 (0.8%), 2 Whites and 1 Native American; Joan, Karen, Laura, Naomi, Pamela, and Victoria, 3 (0.8%) each, and each is White; and Regina, 3, (0.8%), 2 Blacks and 1 White. Also, there are 25 names that appeared two times each: Alice, Alison, Andrea, Anne, Beth, Carol, Dorothy, Eva, Heidi, Jacqueline, Jane, Julia, Kay, Kelly, Linda, Nicole, Sandra, Sharon, and Tara, all White; Cheryl, Dawn, and Mimi, each 1 Asian and 1 White; Danielle, 1 Black and 1 White; Katherine and Leslie, each 1 Native American and 1 White (Table 3a).

For the male Fellows, Table 3b shows that the following names appeared 4 times or more:John, 35, (5.5%), including 30 Whites and 5 Blacks; David, 33 (5.2%), including 31 Whites and 2 Blacks; Robert, 22 (3.5%), including 20 Whites and 2 Blacks; Michael, 19 (3%), all White; Peter and Richard, each 17, (2.7%), all White; William, 15 (2.4%), including 12 Whites and 3 Blacks; Charles, 11 (1.8%), including 9 Whites and 2 Blacks; James, 11 (1.7%), including 10 Whites and 1 Black; Paul, 10 (1.6%), all White; George, 8 (1.3%), including 6 Whites and 2 Blacks; Mark, 8 (1.3%), including 7 Whites and 1 Black; Stephen, 8 (1.3%), including 7 Whites and 1 Asian; Thomas, 7 (1.1%), including 6 Whites and 1 Black; Daniel and Matthew, each 6 (0.9%), all White; Joseph, 6 (0.9%), including 5 Whites and 1 Black; Christopher and Gary, each 5 (0.8%), all White; Bill, Edward, and Jay, each 4 (0.6%), including 3 Whites and 1 Black for each; and Carl, Eric, and Jonathan, each 4 (0.6%), all White. In addition, 15 names appeared 3 times each: Aaron, 2 Blacks and 1 White; Allan, Andrew, Erik, Frank, Gregory, Joel, Jon, Kevin, Philip, Steven, all White; Donald, Henry, Martin, and Walter, each 2 Whites and 1 Black; and Stanley, 1 White and 2 Blacks. Finally, 43 names appeared two times each. (Table 3b).

Table 3a. First Names of MacArthur Female Fellows, 1981 to 2018

| First Name | # | % | White | Black | Asian | Native American |
|---|---|---|---|---|---|---|
| Ada | 1 | 0.3 | 1 | | | |
| Adrian | 1 | 0.3 | 1 | | | |
| Adrienne | 1 | 0.3 | 1 | | | |
| Ai-jen | 1 | 0.3 | | | 1 | |
| Alex | 1 | 0.3 | 1 | | | |
| Alice | 2 | 0.5 | 2 | | | |
| Alicia | 1 | 0.3 | 1 | | | |
| Alisa | 1 | 0.3 | 1 | | | |
| Alison | 2 | 0.5 | 2 | | | |
| Allison | 1 | 0.3 | 1 | | | |
| Alma | 1 | 0.3 | 1 | | | |
| Amalia | 1 | 0.3 | 1 | | | |
| Aminah | 1 | 0.3 | | 1 | | |
| Amy | 4 | 1.1 | 4 | | | |
| An-My | 1 | 0.3 | | | 1 | |
| Ana | 1 | 0.3 | 1 | | | |
| Andrea | 2 | 0.5 | 2 | | | |
| Angela | 3 | 0.8 | 1 | 1 | 1 | |
| Ann | 4 | 1.1 | 4 | | | |
| Anna | 4 | 1.1 | 3 | 1 | | |
| Anne | 2 | 0.5 | 2 | | | |
| Annette | 1 | 0.3 | | 1 | | |
| Annie | 1 | 0.3 | 1 | | | |
| Ayesha | 1 | 0.3 | | | 1 | |

| Name | | | | | | |
|---|---|---|---|---|---|---|
| Barbara | 3 | 0.8 | 2 | 1 | | |
| Becca | 1 | 0.3 | 1 | | | |
| Bernadette | 1 | 0.3 | 1 | | | |
| Bernice | 1 | 0.3 | | 1 | | |
| Beth | 2 | 0.5 | 2 | | | |
| Betsy | 1 | 0.3 | 1 | | | |
| Bette | 1 | 0.3 | 1 | | | |
| Billie | 1 | 0.3 | | 1 | | |
| Bonnie | 1 | 0.3 | 1 | | | |
| Brackette | 1 | 0.3 | | 1 | | |
| Byllye | 1 | 0.3 | | 1 | | |
| Camille | 1 | 0.3 | 1 | | | |
| Carol | 2 | 0.5 | 2 | | | |
| Caroline | 1 | 0.3 | 1 | | | |
| Carolyn | 3 | 0.8 | 3 | | | |
| Carrie | 1 | 0.3 | | 1 | | |
| Cecilia | 1 | 0.3 | 1 | | | |
| Charlotte | 1 | 0.3 | 1 | | | |
| Cheryl | 2 | 0.5 | 1 | | 1 | |
| Chimamanda | 1 | 0.3 | | 1 | | |
| Cindy | 1 | 0.3 | 1 | | | |
| Claire | 5 | 1.3 | 5 | | | |
| Claudia | 1 | 0.3 | | 1 | | |
| Corrine | 1 | 0.3 | 1 | | | |
| Cristina | 1 | 0.3 | 1 | | | |
| Cynthia | 1 | 0.3 | 1 | | | |
| Daisy | 1 | 0.3 | 1 | | | |
| Daniela | 1 | 0.3 | 1 | | | |
| Danielle | 2 | 0.5 | 1 | 1 | | |
| Daphne | 1 | 0.3 | 1 | | | |
| Dawn | 2 | 0.5 | 1 | | 1 | |
| Deborah | 6 | 1.6 | 4 | 1 | 1 | |
| Diane | 1 | 0.3 | 1 | | | |
| Dianne | 1 | 0.3 | 1 | | | |
| Dina | 1 | 0.3 | 1 | | | |

| | | | | | | |
|---|---|---|---|---|---|---|
| Dominique | 1 | 0.3 | | 1 | | |
| Donella | 1 | 0.3 | 1 | | | |
| Doris | 1 | 0.3 | | | 1 | |
| Dorothy | 2 | 0.5 | 2 | | | |
| Edet | 1 | 0.3 | 1 | | | |
| Edith | 1 | 0.3 | 1 | | | |
| Edwidge | 1 | 0.3 | | 1 | | |
| Eiko | 1 | 0.3 | | | 1 | |
| Elaine | 1 | 0.3 | 1 | | | |
| Eleanor | 1 | 0.3 | 1 | | | |
| Elinor | 1 | 0.3 | 1 | | | |
| Elissa | 1 | 0.3 | 1 | | | |
| Elizabeth | 5 | 1.3 | 5 | | | |
| Ellen | 4 | 1.1 | 3 | 1 | | |
| Ellendea | 1 | 0.3 | 1 | | | |
| Elma | 1 | 0.3 | | 1 | | |
| Elodie | 1 | 0.3 | 1 | | | |
| Elouise | 1 | 0.3 | | | | 1 |
| Elyn | 1 | 0.3 | 1 | | | |
| Emily | 1 | 0.3 | 1 | | | |
| Esther | 1 | 0.3 | 1 | | | |
| Eva | 2 | 0.5 | 2 | | | |
| Eve | 1 | 0.3 | | 1 | | |
| Evelyn | 1 | 0.3 | 1 | | | |
| Faye | 1 | 0.3 | 1 | | | |
| Francesca | 1 | 0.3 | 1 | | | |
| Gay | 1 | 0.3 | | 1 | | |
| Geraldine | 1 | 0.3 | 1 | | | |
| Gina | 1 | 0.3 | 1 | | | |
| Gretchen | 1 | 0.3 | 1 | | | |
| Heather | 4 | 1.1 | 4 | | | |
| Heidi | 2 | 0.5 | 2 | | | |
| Helen | 1 | 0.3 | 1 | | | |

| Name | | | | | | |
|---|---|---|---|---|---|---|
| Ida | 1 | 0.3 | 1 | | | |
| Ingrid | 1 | 0.3 | 1 | | | |
| Irene | 1 | 0.3 | 1 | | | |
| Jacqueline | 2 | 0.5 | 2 | | | |
| Jane | 2 | 0.5 | 2 | | | |
| Janet | 1 | 0.3 | 1 | | | |
| Janine | 3 | 0.8 | 2 | | | 1 |
| Jean | 1 | 0.3 | 1 | | | |
| Jeanne | 1 | 0.3 | 1 | | | |
| Jennifer | 5 | 1.3 | 3 | 2 | | |
| Jeraldyne | 1 | 0.3 | 1 | | | |
| Jesmyn | 1 | 0.3 | | 1 | | |
| Jessie | 1 | 0.3 | | | | 1 |
| Jill | 1 | 0.3 | 1 | | | |
| Jillian | 1 | 0.3 | 1 | | | |
| Joan | 3 | 0.8 | 3 | | | |
| Joanna | 1 | 0.3 | 1 | | | |
| Jorie | 1 | 0.3 | 1 | | | |
| Joyce | 1 | 0.3 | | 1 | | |
| Judith | 1 | 0.3 | 1 | | | |
| Judy | 1 | 0.3 | 1 | | | |
| Julia | 2 | 0.5 | 2 | | | |
| Julie | 6 | 1.6 | 4 | 1 | 1 | |
| Kara | 1 | 0.3 | 1 | | | |
| Karen | 3 | 0.8 | 3 | | | |
| Kate | 1 | 0.3 | 1 | | | |
| Katherine | 2 | 0.5 | 1 | | | 1 |
| Kathleen | 1 | 0.3 | 1 | | | |
| Kay | 2 | 0.5 | 2 | | | |
| Kellie | 1 | 0.3 | | 1 | | |
| Kelly | 2 | 0.5 | 2 | | | |
| Kirsten | 1 | 0.3 | 1 | | | |
| Kristina | 1 | 0.3 | 1 | | | |
| Lateefah | 1 | 0.3 | | 1 | | |
| LaToya | 1 | 0.3 | | 1 | | |

| Name | | | | | | |
|---|---|---|---|---|---|---|
| Laura | 3 | 0.8 | 3 | | | |
| Laurel | 1 | 0.3 | 1 | | | |
| Lauren | 1 | 0.3 | 1 | | | |
| Leah | 1 | 0.3 | 1 | | | |
| Lee | 1 | 0.3 | 1 | | | |
| Leila | 1 | 0.3 | 1 | | | |
| Lene | 1 | 0.3 | 1 | | | |
| Leslie | 2 | 0.5 | 1 | | | 1 |
| Lin | 1 | 0.3 | | | 1 | |
| Linda | 2 | 0.5 | 2 | | | |
| Lisa | 4 | 1.1 | 2 | 2 | | |
| Livia | 1 | 0.3 | 1 | | | |
| Liz | 1 | 0.3 | 1 | | | |
| Liza | 1 | 0.3 | 1 | | | |
| Lorna | 1 | 0.3 | 1 | | | |
| Lu | 1 | 0.3 | | | 1 | |
| Lucia | 1 | 0.3 | 1 | | | |
| Lucy | 1 | 0.3 | 1 | | | |
| Lydia | 1 | 0.3 | 1 | | | |
| Lynn | 1 | 0.3 | | 1 | | |
| Lynsey | 1 | 0.3 | 1 | | | |
| Maggie | 1 | 0.3 | 1 | | | |
| Majora | 1 | 0.3 | | 1 | | |
| Margaret | 5 | 1.3 | 5 | | | |
| Mari Jo | 1 | 0.3 | 1 | | | |
| Maria | 4 | 1.1 | 4 | | | |
| Marian | 1 | 0.3 | | 1 | | |
| Marie-Therese | 1 | 0.3 | 1 | | | |
| Marin | 1 | 0.3 | 1 | | | |
| Marina | 1 | 0.3 | 1 | | | |
| Marion | 1 | 0.3 | | 1 | | |
| Marla | 1 | 0.3 | 1 | | | |
| Martha | 1 | 0.3 | 1 | | | |

| Name | | | | | |
|---|---|---|---|---|---|
| Mary | 5 | 1.3 | 4 | 1 | | |
| Melanie | 1 | 0.3 | 1 | | | |
| Melody | 1 | 0.3 | 1 | | | |
| Mercedes | 1 | 0.3 | 1 | | | |
| Meredith | 1 | 0.3 | 1 | | | |
| Michal | 1 | 0.3 | 1 | | | |
| Michelle | 1 | 0.3 | 1 | | | |
| Mimi | 2 | 0.5 | 1 | | 1 | |
| Muriel | 1 | 0.3 | | 1 | | |
| My | 1 | 0.3 | | | 1 | |
| Nancy | 7 | 1.9 | 7 | | | |
| Naomi | 3 | 0.8 | 3 | | | |
| Natalia | 1 | 0.3 | 1 | | | |
| Natalie | 1 | 0.3 | | | | 1 |
| Nawal | 1 | 0.3 | | 1 | | |
| Nergis | 1 | 0.3 | | | 1 | |
| Nicole | 2 | 0.5 | 2 | | | |
| Nikole | 1 | 0.3 | | 1 | | |
| Njideka | 1 | 0.3 | | 1 | | |
| Nora | 1 | 0.3 | 1 | | | |
| Octavia | 1 | 0.3 | | 1 | | |
| Ofelia | 1 | 0.3 | | | | 1 |
| Okwui | 1 | 0.3 | | 1 | | |
| Olufunmilayo | 1 | 0.3 | | 1 | | |
| Pam | 1 | 0.3 | 1 | | | |
| Pamela | 3 | 0.8 | 3 | | | |
| Patricia | 6 | 1.6 | 4 | 1 | | 1 |
| Paule | 1 | 0.3 | | 1 | | |
| Rachel | 1 | 0.3 | 1 | | | |
| Randall | 1 | 0.3 | 1 | | | |
| Rebecca | 6 | 1.6 | 6 | | | |
| Regina | 3 | 0.8 | 1 | 2 | | |
| Rhiannon | 1 | 0.3 | | 1 | | |
| Rita | 1 | 0.3 | 1 | | | |
| Robin | 1 | 0.3 | 1 | | | |

| | | | | | | |
|---|---|---|---|---|---|---|
| Rosalind | 1 | 0.3 | 1 | | | |
| Rosanne | 1 | 0.3 | 1 | | | |
| Ruth | 4 | 1.1 | 4 | | | |
| Sally | 1 | 0.3 | 1 | | | |
| Sandra | 2 | 0.5 | 2 | | | |
| Sandy | 1 | 0.3 | 1 | | | |
| Sara | 3 | 0.8 | 2 | 1 | | |
| Sarah | 7 | 1.9 | 7 | | | |
| Shahzia | 1 | 0.3 | | | 1 | |
| Shannon | 1 | 0.3 | 1 | | | |
| Sharon | 2 | 0.5 | 2 | | | |
| Sheila | 1 | 0.3 | 1 | | | |
| Shelly | 1 | 0.3 | 1 | | | |
| Sherry | 1 | 0.3 | 1 | | | |
| Shirley | 1 | 0.3 | 1 | | | |
| Sophia | 1 | 0.3 | | 1 | | |
| Sue | 1 | 0.3 | 1 | | | |
| Susan | 11 | 2.9 | 11 | | | |
| Suzan-Lori | 1 | 0.3 | | 1 | | |
| Suzanne | 1 | 0.3 | 1 | | | |
| Sylvia | 1 | 0.3 | 1 | | | |
| Tami | 1 | 0.3 | 1 | | | |
| Tara | 2 | 0.5 | 2 | | | |
| Teresita | 1 | 0.3 | 1 | | | |
| Terry | 1 | 0.3 | 1 | | | |
| Thylias | 1 | 0.3 | | 1 | | |
| Tina | 1 | 0.3 | 1 | | | |
| Tiya | 1 | 0.3 | | 1 | | |
| Toba | 1 | 0.3 | 1 | | | |
| Trisha | 1 | 0.3 | 1 | | | |
| Twyla | 1 | 0.3 | 1 | | | |
| Unita | 1 | 0.3 | 1 | | | |
| Uta | 1 | 0.3 | 1 | | | |

| First Name | # | % | White | Black | Asian | Native American |
|---|---|---|---|---|---|---|
| Victoria | 3 | 0.8 | 3 | | | |
| Vija | 1 | 0.3 | 1 | | | |
| Virginia | 1 | 0.3 | | 1 | | |
| Vivian | 1 | 0.3 | 1 | | | |
| Vonnie | 1 | 0.3 | | 1 | | |
| Wafaa | 1 | 0.3 | 1 | | | |
| Wendy | 1 | 0.3 | 1 | | | |
| Wilma | 1 | 0.3 | 1 | | | |
| Wu | 1 | 0.3 | 1 | | | |
| Xiaowei | 1 | 0.3 | | | 1 | |
| Yiyun | 1 | 0.3 | | | 1 | |
| Yoky | 1 | 0.3 | | | 1 | |
| Yukiko | 1 | 0.3 | | | 1 | |
| Yvonne | 1 | 0.3 | 1 | | | |
| Total | 377 | 100 | 295 | 54 | 20 | 8 |

Source: Compiled and computed based on data provided by the MacArthur Fellows Program (June 2017 to February 2019) at: https://www.macfound.org/fellows/search/all.

## Table 3b. First Names of MacArthur Male Fellows, 1981 to 2018

| First Name | # | % | White | Black | Asian | Native American |
|---|---|---|---|---|---|---|
| Aaron | 3 | 0.5 | 1 | 2 | | |
| Adam | 1 | 0.2 | 1 | | | |
| Adrian | 1 | 0.2 | 1 | | | |
| Ahilan | 1 | 0.2 | | | 1 | |
| Alan | 1 | 0.2 | 1 | | | |
| Alar | 1 | 0.2 | 1 | | | |
| Albert | 1 | 0.2 | 1 | | | |
| Aleksandar | 1 | 0.2 | 1 | | | |
| Alex | 1 | 0.2 | 1 | | | |
| Alexander | 1 | 0.2 | 1 | | | |
| Alexei | 2 | 0.3 | 2 | | | |
| Alfonso | 1 | 0.2 | | | | 1 |
| Alfredo | 1 | 0.2 | 1 | | | |

| | | | | | | |
|---|---|---|---|---|---|---|
| Ali | 1 | 0.2 | | | 1 | |
| Allan | 3 | 0.5 | 3 | | | |
| Allen | 1 | 0.2 | 1 | | | |
| Alvin | 1 | 0.2 | 1 | | | |
| Amir | 1 | 0.2 | 1 | | | |
| Amory | 1 | 0.2 | 1 | | | |
| Amos | 1 | 0.2 | 1 | | | |
| Anders | 1 | 0.2 | 1 | | | |
| Andre | 1 | 0.2 | 1 | | | |
| Andrew | 3 | 0.5 | 3 | | | |
| Anthony | 2 | 0.3 | 2 | | | |
| Archie | 1 | 0.2 | 1 | | | |
| Arnaldo | 1 | 0.2 | 1 | | | |
| Arnold | 2 | 0.3 | 1 | 1 | | |
| Arthur | 2 | 0.3 | 1 | 1 | | |
| Attipate | 1 | 0.2 | | | 1 | |
| Atul | 1 | 0.2 | | | 1 | |
| Avner | 1 | 0.2 | 1 | | | |
| Baldemar | 1 | 0.2 | 1 | | | |
| Basil | 1 | 0.2 | 1 | | | |
| Beaumont | 1 | 0.2 | 1 | | | |
| Béla | 1 | 0.2 | 1 | | | |
| Ben | 2 | 0.3 | 2 | | | |
| Benedict | 1 | 0.2 | 1 | | | |
| Benjamin | 2 | 0.3 | 2 | | | |
| Benoît | 1 | 0.2 | 1 | | | |
| Bill | 4 | 0.6 | 3 | 1 | | |
| Brad | 1 | 0.2 | 1 | | | |
| Bradley | 1 | 0.2 | 1 | | | |
| Branden | 1 | 0.2 | | 1 | | |
| Bret | 1 | 0.2 | 1 | | | |
| Brian | 1 | 0.2 | 1 | | | |
| Bright | 1 | 0.2 | | | 1 | |

| | | | | | | |
|---|---|---|---|---|---|---|
| Brooks | 1 | 0.2 | 1 | | | |
| Bruce | 2 | 0.3 | 2 | | | |
| Bryan | 1 | 0.2 | | 1 | | |
| Calvin | 1 | 0.2 | | 1 | | |
| Camilo | 1 | 0.2 | 1 | | | |
| Campbell | 1 | 0.2 | 1 | | | |
| Carl | 4 | 0.6 | 4 | | | |
| Carlos | 1 | 0.2 | 1 | | | |
| Cecil | 1 | 0.2 | | 1 | | |
| Charles | 11 | 1.7 | 9 | 2 | | |
| Christopher | 5 | 0.8 | 5 | | | |
| Clifford | 1 | 0.2 | 1 | | | |
| Colin | 1 | 0.2 | 1 | | | |
| Colson | 1 | 0.2 | | 1 | | |
| Conlon | 1 | 0.2 | 1 | | | |
| Corey | 1 | 0.2 | | 1 | | |
| Cormac | 1 | 0.2 | 1 | | | |
| Cornell | 1 | 0.2 | 1 | | | |
| Craig | 2 | 0.3 | 2 | | | |
| Curtis | 1 | 0.2 | 1 | | | |
| Dafnis | 1 | 0.2 | | 1 | | |
| Damon | 1 | 0.2 | 1 | | | |
| Daniel | 6 | 0.9 | 6 | | | |
| Daryl | 2 | 0.3 | 1 | | | 1 |
| Dave | 1 | 0.2 | 1 | | | |
| David | 33 | 5.2 | 31 | 2 | | |
| Dawoud | 1 | 0.2 | | 1 | | |
| Demetrios | 1 | 0.2 | 1 | | | |
| Dennis | 1 | 0.2 | 1 | | | |
| Derek | 2 | 0.3 | 1 | 1 | | |
| Dimitri | 1 | 0.2 | 1 | | | |
| Dinaw | 1 | 0.2 | | 1 | | |
| Dirk | 1 | 0.2 | 1 | | | |
| Donald | 3 | 0.5 | 2 | 1 | | |
| Douglas | 2 | 0.3 | 2 | | | |

| Name | | | | | |
|---|---|---|---|---|---|
| Drew | 1 | 0.2 | 1 | | |
| Dylan | 1 | 0.2 | | 1 | |
| Eddie | 1 | 0.2 | | 1 | |
| Edgar | 1 | 0.2 | 1 | | |
| Edward | 4 | 0.6 | 3 | 1 | |
| Edwin | 1 | 0.2 | 1 | | |
| Eliot | 1 | 0.2 | 1 | | |
| Elliot | 1 | 0.2 | 1 | | |
| Emmanuel | 2 | 0.3 | 2 | | |
| Eric | 4 | 0.6 | 4 | | |
| Erik | 3 | 0.5 | 3 | | |
| Ernest | 1 | 0.2 | | 1 | |
| Ernesto | 1 | 0.2 | 1 | | |
| Errol | 1 | 0.2 | 1 | | |
| Fazal | 1 | 0.2 | 1 | | |
| Fouad | 1 | 0.2 | 1 | | |
| Francisco | 1 | 0.2 | 1 | | |
| Frank | 3 | 0.5 | 3 | | |
| Franklin | 1 | 0.2 | 1 | | |
| Fred | 1 | 0.2 | | 1 | |
| Frederick | 2 | 0.3 | 2 | | |
| Fritz | 1 | 0.2 | 1 | | |
| Gabriel | 1 | 0.2 | 1 | | |
| Galway | 1 | 0.2 | 1 | | |
| Gary | 5 | 0.8 | 5 | | |
| Geerat | 1 | 0.2 | 1 | | |
| Gene | 1 | 0.2 | | | 1 |
| George | 8 | 1.3 | 6 | 2 | |
| Getatchew | 1 | 0.2 | | 1 | |
| Greg | 1 | 0.2 | 1 | | |
| Gregg | 1 | 0.2 | 1 | | |
| Gregory | 3 | 0.5 | 3 | | |
| Guillermo | 2 | 0.3 | 2 | | |

| | | | | | | |
|---|---|---|---|---|---|---|
| Günter | 1 | 0.2 | 1 | | | |
| Gunther | 1 | 0.2 | 1 | | | |
| Guy | 2 | 0.3 | 2 | | | |
| Han | 1 | 0.2 | | | 1 | |
| Harlan | 1 | 0.2 | 1 | | | |
| Harold | 1 | 0.2 | 1 | | | |
| Henry | 3 | 0.5 | 2 | 1 | | |
| Hideo | 1 | 0.2 | | | 1 | |
| Hipolito | 1 | 0.2 | 1 | | | |
| Horace | 1 | 0.2 | 1 | | | |
| Horng-Tzer | 1 | 0.2 | | | 1 | |
| Howard | 1 | 0.2 | 1 | | | |
| Hugo | 1 | 0.2 | 1 | | | |
| Huynh | 1 | 0.2 | | | 1 | |
| Ian | 1 | 0.2 | 1 | | | |
| Iñigo | 1 | 0.2 | 1 | | | |
| Ira | 1 | 0.2 | 1 | | | |
| Irving | 2 | 0.3 | 2 | | | |
| Ishmael | 1 | 0.2 | | 1 | | |
| Israel | 1 | 0.2 | 1 | | | |
| Ivan | 1 | 0.2 | 1 | | | |
| Jack | 2 | 0.3 | 2 | | | |
| Jacob | 2 | 0.3 | 2 | | | |
| Jacques | 1 | 0.2 | 1 | | | |
| Jad | 1 | 0.2 | 1 | | | |
| James | 11 | 1.7 | 10 | 1 | | |
| Jared | 1 | 0.2 | 1 | | | |
| Jason | 2 | 0.3 | 1 | 1 | | |
| Jay | 4 | 0.6 | 3 | 1 | | |
| Jed | 1 | 0.2 | 1 | | | |
| Jeffrey | 2 | 0.3 | 2 | | | |
| Jeremy | 1 | 0.2 | 1 | | | |
| Jerry | 1 | 0.2 | 1 | | | |
| Jerzy | 1 | 0.2 | 1 | | | |
| Jim | 2 | 0.3 | 1 | | 1 | |

| Name | | | | | |
|---|---|---|---|---|---|
| Jin-Quan | 1 | 0.2 | | | 1 | |
| Joaquin | 1 | 0.2 | 1 | | | |
| Joel | 3 | 0.5 | 3 | | | |
| John | 35 | 5.5 | 30 | 5 | | |
| Jon | 3 | 0.5 | 3 | | | |
| Jonathan | 4 | 0.6 | 4 | | | |
| Jorge | 1 | 0.2 | 1 | | | |
| José | 2 | 0.3 | 2 | | | |
| Joseph | 6 | 1.0 | 5 | 1 | | |
| Josh | 1 | 0.2 | 1 | | | |
| Joshua | 1 | 0.2 | 1 | | | |
| Josiah | 1 | 0.2 | 1 | | | |
| Juan | 2 | 0.3 | 1 | 1 | | |
| Junot | 1 | 0.2 | | 1 | | |
| Karl | 1 | 0.2 | 1 | | | |
| Kartik | 1 | 0.2 | | | 1 | |
| Ken | 2 | 0.3 | 2 | | | |
| Kenneth | 1 | 0.2 | 1 | | | |
| Kent | 1 | 0.2 | 1 | | | |
| Kerry | 1 | 0.2 | | 1 | | |
| Kevin | 3 | 0.5 | 3 | | | |
| Khaled | 1 | 0.2 | 1 | | | |
| Koma | 1 | 0.2 | | | 1 | |
| Kun-Liang | 1 | 0.2 | | | 1 | |
| Kyle | 1 | 0.2 | | 1 | | |
| Lakshminarayanan | 1 | 0.2 | | | 1 | |
| Lawrence | 2 | 0.3 | 2 | | | |
| Lee | 2 | 0.3 | 2 | | | |
| Leo | 2 | 0.3 | 2 | | | |
| Leonard | 2 | 0.3 | 2 | | | |
| Lester | 1 | 0.2 | 1 | | | |
| Leszek | 1 | 0.2 | 1 | | | |
| Lewis | 1 | 0.2 | 1 | | | |

| | | | | | | |
|---|---|---|---|---|---|---|
| Lin-Manuel | 1 | 0.2 | 1 | | | |
| Loïc | 1 | 0.2 | 1 | | | |
| Loren | 1 | 0.2 | 1 | | | |
| Lorenz | 1 | 0.2 | 1 | | | |
| Louis | 1 | 0.2 | | 1 | | |
| Luis | 2 | 0.3 | 2 | | | |
| Maneesh | 1 | 0.2 | | | 1 | |
| Manu | 1 | 0.2 | | | 1 | |
| Marc | 2 | 0.3 | 2 | | | |
| Marcel | 1 | 0.2 | 1 | | | |
| Marin | 1 | 0.2 | 1 | | | |
| Mark | 8 | 1.3 | 7 | 1 | | |
| Markus | 1 | 0.2 | 1 | | | |
| Martin | 3 | 0.5 | 2 | 1 | | |
| Marvin | 1 | 0.2 | 1 | | | |
| Matias | 1 | 0.2 | 1 | | | |
| Matthew | 6 | 0.9 | 6 | | | |
| Maurice | 1 | 0.2 | | | 1 | |
| Maxwell | 1 | 0.2 | | 1 | | |
| Merce | 1 | 0.2 | 1 | | | |
| Meyer | 1 | 0.2 | 1 | | | |
| Michael | 19 | 3.0 | 19 | | | |
| Miguel | 1 | 0.2 | 1 | | | |
| Milton | 1 | 0.2 | 1 | | | |
| Mitchell | 1 | 0.2 | 1 | | | |
| Morton | 1 | 0.2 | 1 | | | |
| Mott | 1 | 0.2 | 1 | | | |
| Nathan | 1 | 0.2 | 1 | | | |
| Ned | 1 | 0.2 | 1 | | | |
| Nicholas | 2 | 0.3 | 2 | | | |
| Noel | 1 | 0.2 | 1 | | | |
| Norman | 2 | 0.3 | 2 | | | |
| Olivier | 1 | 0.2 | 1 | | | |
| Ornette | 1 | 0.2 | | 1 | | |
| Osvaldo | 1 | 0.2 | 1 | | | |

| Otis | 1 | 0.2 | | 1 | | |
| Patrick | 2 | 0.3 | 1 | 1 | | |
| Paul | 10 | 1.6 | 10 | | | |
| Pedro | 2 | 0.3 | 2 | | | |
| Pehr | 1 | 0.2 | 1 | | | |
| Peidong | 1 | 0.2 | | | 1 | |
| Pepon | 1 | 0.2 | | 1 | | |
| Persi | 1 | 0.2 | 1 | | | |
| Peter | 17 | 2.7 | 17 | | | |
| Phil | 1 | 0.2 | 1 | | | |
| Philip | 3 | 0.5 | 3 | | | |
| Rackstraw | 1 | 0.2 | 1 | | | |
| Raj | 2 | 0.3 | | | 2 | |
| Ralf | 1 | 0.2 | 1 | | | |
| Ralph | 2 | 0.3 | 2 | | | |
| Rami | 1 | 0.2 | 1 | | | |
| Ramón | 1 | 0.2 | 1 | | | |
| Ran | 1 | 0.2 | 1 | | | |
| Randolph | 1 | 0.2 | 1 | | | |
| Raphael | 1 | 0.2 | 1 | | | |
| Raymond | 1 | 0.2 | 1 | | | |
| Reginald | 1 | 0.2 | | 1 | | |
| Ricardo | 1 | 0.2 | 1 | | | |
| Richard | 17 | 0.3 | 17 | | | |
| Rick | 1 | 0.2 | | 1 | | |
| Robert | 22 | 3.5 | 20 | 2 | | |
| Roger | 1 | 0.2 | 1 | | | |
| Rogers | 1 | 0.2 | 1 | | | |
| Roland | 1 | 0.2 | | 1 | | |
| Roy | 1 | 0.2 | 1 | | | |
| Rueben | 1 | 0.2 | 1 | | | |
| Russell | 1 | 0.2 | 1 | | | |
| Sam | 1 | 0.2 | 1 | | | |

| Name | | | | | | |
|---|---|---|---|---|---|---|
| Sam-Ang | 1 | 0.2 | | | 1 | |
| Samuel | 2 | 0.3 | 2 | | | |
| Sarkis | 1 | 0.2 | 1 | | | |
| Saul | 2 | 0.3 | 2 | | | |
| Sebastian | 1 | 0.2 | 1 | | | |
| Sendhil | 1 | 0.2 | | | 1 | |
| Sergiu | 1 | 0.2 | 1 | | | |
| Seweryn | 1 | 0.2 | 1 | | | |
| Shawn | 1 | 0.2 | 1 | | | |
| Shelly | 1 | 0.2 | 1 | | | |
| Shelomo | 1 | 0.2 | 1 | | | |
| Shen | 1 | 0.2 | | | 1 | |
| Shing-Tung | 1 | 0.2 | | | 1 | |
| Shwetak | 1 | 0.2 | | | 1 | |
| Sidney | 2 | 0.3 | 2 | | | |
| Sokoni | 1 | 0.2 | | 1 | | |
| Stanley | 3 | 0.5 | 1 | 2 | | |
| Stefan | 1 | 0.2 | 1 | | | |
| Stephen | 8 | 1.3 | 7 | | 1 | |
| Steve | 1 | 0.2 | | 1 | | |
| Steven | 3 | 0.5 | 3 | | | |
| Stewart | 1 | 0.2 | | | 1 | |
| Stuart | 2 | 0.3 | 2 | | | |
| Subhash | 1 | 0.2 | | | 1 | |
| Sunil | 1 | 0.2 | | | 1 | |
| Sven | 1 | 0.2 | | | | 1 |
| Ta-Nehisi | 1 | 0.2 | | 1 | | |
| Tarell | 1 | 0.2 | | 1 | | |
| Taylor | 2 | 0.3 | 2 | | | |
| Ted | 1 | 0.2 | 1 | | | |
| Terence | 1 | 0.2 | | | 1 | |
| Terrance | 1 | 0.2 | | 1 | | |
| Terry | 1 | 0.2 | 1 | | | |
| Theodore | 2 | 0.3 | 2 | | | |
| Thom | 1 | 0.2 | 1 | | | |

| | | | | | | |
|---|---|---|---|---|---|---|
| Thomas | 7 | 1.1 | 6 | 1 | | |
| Tim | 1 | 0.2 | 1 | | | |
| Timothy | 1 | 0.2 | 1 | | | |
| Titus | 1 | 0.2 | | 1 | | |
| Todd | 1 | 0.2 | 1 | | | |
| Tom | 1 | 0.2 | 1 | | | |
| Tommie | 1 | 0.2 | | 1 | | |
| Trevor | 1 | 0.2 | 1 | | | |
| Trimpin (Gerhard) | 1 | 0.2 | 1 | | | |
| Tyshawn | 1 | 0.2 | | 1 | | |
| Ubaldo | 1 | 0.2 | 1 | | | |
| Valery | 1 | 0.2 | 1 | | | |
| Vamsi | 1 | 0.2 | | | 1 | |
| Ved | 1 | 0.2 | | | 1 | |
| Viet | 1 | 0.2 | | | 1 | |
| Vijay | 2 | 0.3 | | | 2 | |
| Vincent | 1 | 0.2 | 1 | | | |
| W.Keith | 1 | 0.2 | 1 | | | |
| Walter | 3 | 0.5 | 2 | 1 | | |
| Wes | 1 | 0.2 | 1 | | | |
| Wesley | 1 | 0.2 | | | | 1 |
| Whitfield | 1 | 0.2 | | 1 | | |
| Will | 1 | 0.2 | | 1 | | |
| William | 15 | 2.4 | 12 | 3 | | |
| Willie | 1 | 0.2 | 1 | | | |
| Xiao | 1 | 0.2 | | | 1 | |
| Xu | 1 | 0.2 | | | 1 | |
| Yitang | 1 | 0.2 | | | 1 | |
| Yuval | 1 | 0.2 | 1 | | | |
| Total | 637 | 100.0 | 520 | 73 | 40 | 4 |

Source: Compiled and computed based on data provided by the MacArthur Fellows Program (June 2017 to February 2019) at: https://www.macfound.org/fellows/search/all.

## Age at the Time of Award of MacArthur Fellows, 1981 to 2018

The age at the time of award data show many similarities and some differences among the sexes/genders and racial groups. According to Table 4, the mean age of all 1,014 MacArthur Fellows selected from 1981 to 2018 is 45.8 years: 45.98 years for men and 45.53 years for women. Asians have the youngest, with a mean age of 41 years, but 38.9 years for Asian women. Black men and Native American women are the oldest, each with a mean age of 47 years. The median age of all Fellows is 44 years: 44 years each for men and women. Asians have the youngest median age at 41 years, with Asian women at 39 years. Black Fellows have the highest median age at 47 years, with Black men at 48 years. Black women and Native American women have the second-highest median age at 45.5 years each. The mode for all Fellows is 40 years, appearing 50 times. The mode for women is 42 years, appearing 21 times; and the modes for men are 38 years and 40 years, each appearing 32 times. Black men have the highest mode, 53 years, appearing six times. The maximum age among all Fellows is 83 years and the minimum age is 18 years (each by a White male). The maximum age for women is 79 years (a White woman) and the minimum age for women is 26 years (a Black woman). Asian women have the lowest maximum age at 52 years. The range for all Fellows is 65 years: 65 years for men and 53 years for women. The standard deviation for the age of all Fellows is 10.33 years: 10.72 years for men and 9.64 years for women. White men have the highest standard deviation at 10.93 years and Asian women have the lowest at 5.1 years (Table 4).

Table 4. Age at Time of Award of MacArthur Fellows, 1981 to 2018

| Variable | Mean | Median | | Maximum | Minimum | | Standard | |
|---|---|---|---|---|---|---|---|---|
| | Age | Age | Mode | Age | Age | Rane | Deviation | N(n) |
| All | 45.8 | 44 | 40 (50 times) | 83 | 18 | 65 | 10.33 | 1014 |
| Men | 45.98 | 44 | 38 & 40 (32 times) | 83 | 18 | 65 | 10.72 | 637 |
| Women | 45.53 | 44 | 42 (21 times) | 79 | 26 | 53 | 9.64 | 377 |
| Asian | 41 | 40 | 44 (6 times) | 69 | 29 | 40 | 8.5 | 60 |
| Asian Men | 42.1 | 41 | 44 (5 times) | 69 | 29 | 40 | 9.62 | 40 |
| Asian Women | 38.9 | 39 | 42 (3 times) | 52 | 31 | 21 | 5.1 | 20 |

| | | | | | | | | |
|---|---|---|---|---|---|---|---|---|
| Black | 46.82 | 47 | 42 (10 times) | 71 | 26 | 45 | 9.97 | 127 |
| Black Men | 47 | 48 | 53 (6 times) | 66 | 30 | 36 | 9.56 | 73 |
| Black Women | 46.57 | 45.5 | 40 & 42 (5 times) | 71 | 26 | 45 | 10.6 | 54 |
| Native American | 45.33 | 45 | 40, 45, & 52 (2 times) | 63 | 32 | 31 | 8.8 | 12 |
| Native American Men | 42 | 41.5 | 32, 40, 43 & 53 | 53 | 32 | 21 | 8.68 | 4 |
| Native American Women | 47 | 45.5 | 45 & 52 (2 times) | 63 | 33 | 30 | 8.94 | 8 |
| White | 46 | 44 | 37 (42 times) | 83 | 18 | 65 | 10.5 | 815 |
| White Men | 46.2 | 44 | 40 (30 times) | 83 | 18 | 65 | 10.93 | 520 |
| White Women | 45.74 | 45 | 37 (16 times) | 79 | 27 | 52 | 9.6 | 295 |

Source: Compiled and computed based on data provided by the MacArthur Fellows Program (June 2017 to February 2019) at: https://www.macfound.org/fellows/search/all.

## Year at Time of Award of MacArthur Fellows, 1981 to 2018

The data for the year at the time of winning the MacArthur Fellows award is very useful because it tells a story of the gradual rise in the numbers of women and minorities who have been selected as Fellows. Table 5 presents data showing the year MacArthur Fellows won their awards. The award years are from each year from 1981 to 2018 and are also grouped into five-year intervals. Table 5 illustrates that the vast majority of Fellows selected in the first decade were men and White. However, starting in the second decade to the present, the numbers of women and minorities increased substantially. For example, in 1981 (the first year), of the 41 individuals selected, men accounted for 35 (85.4%) and women accounted for 6 (14.6%). Whites accounted for 36 (87.8%), and White men accounted for 32 (78%). No Asian was selected in 1981; 4 Blacks (3 men and 1 woman); and 1 Native American woman were selected. From 1981 to 1985, of the 164 individuals selected, men accounted for 140 (85.4%) and women accounted for 24 (14.6%). Whites accounted for 150 (91.5%), with White men accounting for 132 (80.5%), and White women accounting for 18 (11%); 9 (5.5%) Blacks (5 women and 4 men); 3 (1.8%) Asians (all men); and 2 (1.2%) Native Americans (1 man and 1 woman).

From the 1990s to 2018, there was a gradual and significant increase in the numbers of women and minorities who won the MacArthur Fellowship, with minorities having higher proportions than their proportions in the general United States population. For example, in 2018, there were 249,193,000 people aged 18 and over in the United States: 128,488,000 (51.6%) women;120,705,000 (48.4%) men; 158,209,000 (63.5%) non-Hispanic Whites; 81,060,000 (32.5%) non-Hispanic White women;77,149,000 (31%) non-Hispanic White men;33,205,000 (13.3%) Blacks; 18,035,000 (7.2%) Black women;15,170,000 (6.1%) Black men;; 15,456,000 (6.2%) Asians; 8,162, 000 (3.3%) Asian women; and 7,294,000 (2.9%) Asian men ("Table 1. Educational Attainment of the Population 18 Years and Over, by Age, Sex, Race, and Hispanic Origin: 2018," 2019). According to the United States Census Bureau, as of 2017, the American Indian and Alaska Native alone population was 2.73 million. Of that total, 1.95 million (73.1%) were 18 years and over: 51.1% women and 48.9% men ("Selected Population Profile in the United States: 2017 American Community Survey 1 Year-Estimates," 2020).

Of the 141 Fellows selected from 1991 to 1995, 61 (43.3%) were women; 26 (18.4%) were minorities, and 21 (14.9%) were Black. Of the 121 Fellows selected from 2006 to 2010, 59 (48.8%) were women; and 32 (26.4%) were minorities. Of the 113 Fellows selected from 2011 to 2015, women accounted for 48 (42.5%); and minorities accounted for 28 (24.8%). Of the 141 Fellows selected from 1991 to 1995, 21 (14.9%) were Black (15 men and 6 women). Of the 119 Fellows selected from 2001 to 2005, 17 (14.3%) were Black (10 women and 7 men); and 9 (7.6%) were Asian (5 men and 4 women). Of the 121 Fellows selected from 2006 to 2010, 17 (14.1%) were Black (9 women and 8 men); 13 (10.7%) were Asian (8 women and 5 men), and 2 (1.7%) were Native American (1 man and 1 woman). Of the 113 Fellows selected from 2011 to 2015, 16 (14.2%) were Black (13 men and 3 women); and 12 (10.6%) were Asian (7 men and 5 women). Finally, of the 119 Fellows selected from 2015 to 2018, 36 (50%) were women; 15 (20.8%) were Black (9 women and 6 men); 10 (13.9%) were Asian (9 men and 1 woman), and 2 (2.8%) were Native American (1 man and 1 woman) (Table 5).

## Table 5. Year at Time of Award of MacArthur Fellows, 1981 to 2018

| Year | Men | Women | White | Men | Women | Black | Men | Women | Asian | Men | Women | Native American | Men | Women |
|---|---|---|---|---|---|---|---|---|---|---|---|---|---|---|
| 1981 | 35 | 6 | 36 | 32 | 4 | 4 | 3 | 1 | | | | 1 | | 1 |
| 1982 | 17 | 1 | 15 | 14 | 1 | 1 | 1 | | 1 | 1 | | 1 | 1 | |
| 1983 | 28 | 6 | 33 | 27 | 6 | | | | 1 | 1 | | | | |
| 1984 | 39 | 7 | 44 | 39 | 5 | 2 | | 2 | | | | | | |
| 1985 | 21 | 4 | 22 | 20 | 2 | 2 | | 2 | 1 | 1 | | | | |
| Total | 140 | 24 | 150 | 132 | 18 | 9 | 4 | 5 | 3 | 3 | 0 | 2 | 1 | 1 |
| 1986 | 23 | 2 | 24 | 22 | 2 | 1 | 1 | | | | | | | |
| 1987 | 28 | 4 | 28 | 25 | 3 | 2 | 1 | 1 | 1 | 1 | | 1 | 1 | |
| 1988 | 23 | 6 | 25 | 19 | 6 | 4 | 4 | | | | | | | |
| 1989 | 20 | 9 | 25 | 18 | 7 | 4 | 2 | 2 | | | | | | |
| 1990 | 23 | 13 | 31 | 19 | 12 | 5 | 4 | 1 | | | | | | |
| Total | 117 | 34 | 133 | 103 | 30 | 16 | 12 | 4 | 1 | 1 | 0 | 1 | 1 | 0 |
| 1991 | 22 | 9 | 25 | 18 | 7 | 4 | 3 | 1 | 1 | 1 | | 1 | | 1 |
| 1992 | 17 | 17 | 31 | 16 | 15 | 3 | 1 | 2 | | | | | | |
| 1993 | 18 | 13 | 24 | 12 | 12 | 6 | 5 | 1 | 1 | 1 | | | | |
| 1994 | 14 | 7 | | 9 | 6 | | 4 | | | 1 | | | | 1 |
| 1995 | 9 | 15 | 20 | 7 | 13 | 2 | 2 | 2 | | | | | | |
| Total | 80 | 61 | 100 | 62 | 53 | 15 | 15 | 6 | 2 | 3 | 0 | 1 | 0 | 2 |
| 1996 | 13 | 8 | 14 | 10 | 4 | 5 | 2 | 3 | 2 | 1 | 1 | | | |
| 1997 | 13 | 10 | 19 | 11 | 8 | 2 | 1 | 1 | 1 | 1 | | 1 | | 1 |
| 1998 | 19 | 12 | 26 | 15 | 11 | 2 | 2 | | 3 | 2 | 1 | | | |
| 1999 | 17 | 15 | 26 | 13 | 13 | 4 | 3 | 1 | 1 | 1 | | 1 | | 1 |
| 2000 | 13 | 13 | 21 | 11 | 10 | 3 | | 3 | 2 | 2 | | | | |
| Total | 75 | 58 | 106 | 60 | 46 | 16 | 8 | 8 | 9 | 7 | 2 | 2 | 0 | 2 |
| 2001 | 12 | 11 | 18 | 10 | 8 | 2 | | 2 | 3 | 2 | 1 | | | |
| 2002 | 14 | 10 | 20 | 10 | 10 | 3 | 3 | | 1 | 1 | | | | |

| Year | | | | | | | | | | | | | | |
|---|---|---|---|---|---|---|---|---|---|---|---|---|---|---|
| 2003 | 12 | 12 | 17 | 11 | 6 | 4 | | 4 | 3 | 1 | 2 | | | |
| 2004 | 10 | 13 | 17 | 6 | 11 | 4 | 3 | 1 | 1 | 1 | | 1 | | 1 |
| 2005 | 14 | 11 | 20 | 13 | 7 | 4 | 1 | 3 | 1 | | 1 | | | |
| Total | 62 | 57 | 92 | 50 | 42 | 17 | 7 | 10 | 9 | 5 | 4 | 1 | 0 | 1 |
| 2006 | 14 | 11 | 19 | 11 | 8 | 3 | 1 | 2 | 3 | 2 | 1 | | | |
| 2007 | 13 | 11 | 15 | 9 | 6 | 4 | 2 | 2 | 4 | 1 | 3 | 1 | 1 | |
| 2008 | 11 | 14 | 20 | 9 | 11 | 5 | 2 | 3 | | | | | | |
| 2009 | 12 | 12 | 19 | 9 | 10 | 2 | 1 | 1 | 3 | 2 | 1 | | | |
| 2010 | 12 | 11 | 16 | 10 | 6 | 3 | 2 | 1 | 3 | | 3 | 1 | | 1 |
| Total | 62 | 59 | 89 | 48 | 41 | 17 | 8 | 9 | 13 | 5 | 8 | 2 | 1 | 1 |
| 2011 | 12 | 9 | 17 | 9 | 8 | 2 | 2 | | 2 | 1 | 1 | | | |
| 2012 | 13 | 10 | 17 | 8 | 9 | 3 | 3 | | 3 | 2 | 1 | | | |
| 2013 | 13 | 11 | 19 | 10 | 9 | 3 | 2 | 1 | 2 | 1 | 1 | | | |
| 2014 | 12 | 9 | 15 | 8 | 7 | 4 | 3 | 1 | 2 | 1 | 1 | | | |
| 2015 | 15 | 9 | 17 | 10 | 7 | 4 | 3 | 1 | 3 | 2 | 1 | | | |
| Total | 65 | 48 | 85 | 45 | 40 | 16 | 13 | 3 | 12 | 7 | 5 | 0 | 0 | 0 |
| 2016 | 11 | 12 | 13 | 4 | 9 | 4 | 1 | 3 | 5 | 5 | | 1 | 1 | |
| 2017 | 15 | 9 | 16 | 11 | 5 | 6 | 2 | 4 | 2 | 2 | | | | |
| 2018 | 10 | 15 | 16 | 5 | 11 | 5 | 3 | 2 | 3 | 2 | 1 | 1 | | 1 |
| Total | 36 | 36 | 45 | 20 | 25 | 15 | 6 | 9 | 10 | 9 | 1 | 2 | 1 | 1 |
| Overall Total | 637 | 377 | 815 | 520 | 295 | 127 | 73 | 54 | 60 | 40 | 20 | 4 | | 8 |

Source: Compiled and computed based on data provided by the MacArthur Fellows Program (June 2017 to February 2019) at: https://www.macfound.org/fellows/search/all.

## U.S. State, U.S. Region, Country, and World Region Where MacArthur Fellows were Located at the Time of Award, 1981 to 2018

The geographic location of an individual when he or she wins the MacArthur Fellowship is a piece of very important information. First, that information can tell us whether a Fellow won the award in the state or country where they were born, especially since the place of birth information is available in this study. Second, the geographic or regional location at the time of award is also important because the level of competition for talent among U.S. states, countries, and world regions is currently very high. These entities are providing various types of incentives to highly talented or skilled individuals to either remain or move to their geographic entity (Campanella, 2015; Kaba 2017a).

Table 6 presents data on the geographic location of MacArthur Fellows at the time they were selected. Of the 1,014 Fellows, data are available for 1,013 (99.9%) of them (data not available for 1 White man). Wooster (2014) presents an explanation of this missing data. Of the 1,013 Fellows, 974 (96.2%) were located in the United States at the time of award, and 39 (3.8%) were located outside of the United States. Of the 974 Fellows located in the United States, 453 (46.5%, but 44.7% of all Fellows) were in the Northeast (including 220 Fellows in New York, 117 in Massachusetts, 47 in New Jersey, 24 in Pennsylvania, 22 in Connecticut, and 10 in Rhode Island); 269 (27.6%, but 26.6% of all Fellows) were in the West (including 195 in California, 19 in Washington, 14 in Arizona, and 13 in Colorado); 135 (13.9%, but 13.3% of all Fellows) in the South (including 36 in Washington, D.C., 16 in Maryland, 14 each in Texas and Virginia, and 11 in North Carolina; and 117 (12%, but 11.5% of all Fellows) were in the Midwest (including 53 in Illinois and 29 in Michigan).

From a racial perspective, of the 1,013 Fellows, 777 (76.7%, but 79.8% of 974 in the U.S.) Whites were located in the United States (496 men and 281 women); 126 (12.4%, but 12.9% of the U.S. total) were Black (72 men and 54 women); 59 (5.8%, but 6.1% of U.S. total) were Asian (39 men and 20 women), and 12 (1.2%, and also 1.2% of U.S. total) were Native American (8 women and 4 men).

Regionally in the United States, of the 777 Whites, 371 (47.8%, but 38.1% of 777 Whites) were located in the Northeast (221 men and 150 women); 218 (28.1%, but 22.4% of U.S. total) were in the West (151 men and 67 women); 100 (12.9%, but 10.3% of U.S. total) were in the South (68 men and 32 women); and 88 (11.3%, but 9% of U.S. total) were in the Midwest (56 men and 32 women).

Of the 39 Fellows who won the Fellowship while outside of the United States, 19 (48.7%) were in Europe (18 Whites (12 men and 6 women) and 1 Asian man). There were 11 Fellows in Western Europe (8 White men, 2 White women, and 1 Asian man); 5 Whites in Northern Europe (3 Women and 2 men); and 3 Whites in Southern Europe (2 men and 1 woman). There were 4 White Fellows in Canada (2 men and 2 women). There were 5 Fellows in Africa (4 White women and 1 Black man). There were 5 White Fellows in Asia (all men). There were 5 Whites in Latin America (3 men and 2 women). Finally, there was 1 White man in Oceania (Australia) (Table 6).

Table 6. U.S. State, U.S. Region, Country, and World Region Where MacArthur Fellows were Located at the Time of Award, 1981 to 2018

| Year | Men | Women | White | Men | Women | Black | Men | Women | Asian | Men | Women | Native American. | Men | Women | Year | Men | Women |
|---|---|---|---|---|---|---|---|---|---|---|---|---|---|---|---|---|---|
| 1981 | 35 | 6 | 36 | 32 | 4 | 4 | 3 | 1 | | | | 1 | | 1 | 1981 | 35 | 6 |
| 1982 | 17 | 1 | 15 | 14 | 1 | 1 | 1 | | 1 | 1 | | 1 | 1 | | 1982 | 17 | 1 |
| 1983 | 28 | 6 | 33 | 27 | 6 | | | | 1 | 1 | | | | | 1983 | 28 | 6 |
| 1984 | 39 | 7 | 44 | 39 | 5 | 2 | | 2 | | | | | | | 1984 | 39 | 7 |
| 1985 | 21 | 4 | 22 | 20 | 2 | 2 | | | 2 | 1 | 1 | | | | 1985 | 21 | 4 |
| Total | 140 | 24 | 150 | 132 | 18 | 9 | 4 | 5 | 3 | 3 | 0 | 2 | 1 | 1 | Total | 140 | 24 |
| 1986 | 23 | 2 | 24 | 22 | 2 | 1 | 1 | | | | | | | | 1986 | 23 | 2 |
| 1987 | 28 | 4 | 28 | 25 | 3 | 2 | 1 | 1 | 1 | 1 | | 1 | 1 | | 1987 | 28 | 4 |
| 1988 | 23 | 6 | 25 | 19 | 6 | 4 | 4 | | | | | | | | 1988 | 23 | 6 |
| 1989 | 20 | 9 | 25 | 18 | 7 | 4 | 2 | 2 | | | | | | | 1989 | 20 | 9 |
| 1990 | 23 | 13 | 31 | 19 | 12 | 5 | 4 | 1 | | | | | | | 1990 | 23 | 13 |
| Total | 117 | 34 | 133 | 103 | 30 | 16 | 12 | 4 | 1 | 1 | 0 | 1 | 1 | 0 | Total | 117 | 34 |
| 1991 | 22 | 9 | 25 | 18 | 7 | 4 | 3 | 1 | 1 | 1 | | 1 | | 1 | 1991 | 22 | 9 |
| 1992 | 17 | 17 | 31 | 16 | 15 | 3 | 1 | 2 | | | | | | | 1992 | 17 | 17 |
| 1993 | 18 | 13 | 24 | 12 | 12 | 6 | 5 | 1 | 1 | 1 | | | | | 1993 | 18 | 13 |
| 1994 | 14 | 7 | 9 | | 6 | | 4 | | | | 1 | | | 1 | 1994 | 14 | 7 |

| | | | | | | | | | | | | | | | |
|---|---|---|---|---|---|---|---|---|---|---|---|---|---|---|---|
| 1995 | 9 | 15 | 20 | 7 | 13 | 2 | 2 | 2 | | | | | | 1995 | 9 |
| Total | 80 | 61 | 100 | 62 | 53 | 15 | 15 | 6 | 2 | 3 | 0 | 1 | 0 | 2 | Total | 80 |
| | | | | | | | | | | | | | | | |
| 1996 | 13 | 8 | 14 | 10 | 4 | 5 | 2 | 3 | 2 | 1 | 1 | | | 1996 | 13 |
| 1997 | 13 | 10 | 19 | 11 | 8 | 2 | 1 | 1 | 1 | 1 | | 1 | | 1 | 1997 | 13 |
| 1998 | 19 | 12 | 26 | 15 | 11 | 2 | 2 | | 3 | 2 | 1 | | | | 1998 | 19 |
| 1999 | 17 | 15 | 26 | 13 | 13 | 4 | 3 | 1 | 1 | 1 | | 1 | | 1 | 1999 | 17 |
| 2000 | 13 | 13 | 21 | 11 | 10 | 3 | | 3 | 2 | 2 | | | | | 2000 | 13 |
| Total | 75 | 58 | 106 | 60 | 46 | 16 | 8 | 8 | 9 | 7 | 2 | 2 | 0 | 2 | Total | 75 |
| | | | | | | | | | | | | | | | |
| 2001 | 12 | 11 | 18 | 10 | 8 | 2 | | 2 | 3 | 2 | 1 | | | | 2001 | 12 |
| 2002 | 14 | 10 | 20 | 10 | 10 | 3 | 3 | | 1 | 1 | | | | | 2002 | 14 |
| 2003 | 12 | 12 | 17 | 11 | 6 | 4 | | 4 | 3 | 1 | 2 | | | | 2003 | 12 |
| 2004 | 10 | 13 | 17 | 6 | 11 | 4 | 3 | 1 | 1 | 1 | | 1 | | 1 | 2004 | 10 |
| 2005 | 14 | 11 | 20 | 13 | 7 | 4 | 1 | 3 | 1 | | 1 | | | | 2005 | 14 |
| Total | 62 | 57 | 92 | 50 | 42 | 17 | 7 | 10 | 9 | 5 | 4 | 1 | 0 | 1 | Total | 62 |
| | | | | | | | | | | | | | | | |
| 2006 | 14 | 11 | 19 | 11 | 8 | 3 | 1 | 2 | 3 | 2 | 1 | | | | 2006 | 14 |
| 2007 | 13 | 11 | 15 | 9 | 6 | 4 | 2 | 2 | 4 | 1 | 3 | 1 | 1 | | 2007 | 13 |
| 2008 | 11 | 14 | 20 | 9 | 11 | 5 | 2 | 3 | | | | | | | 2008 | 11 |
| 2009 | 12 | 12 | 19 | 9 | 10 | 2 | 1 | 1 | 3 | 2 | 1 | | | | 2009 | 12 |
| 2010 | 12 | 11 | 16 | 10 | 6 | 3 | 2 | 1 | 3 | | 3 | 1 | | 1 | 2010 | 12 |
| Total | 62 | 59 | 89 | 48 | 41 | 17 | 8 | 9 | 13 | 5 | 8 | 2 | 1 | 1 | Total | 62 |
| | | | | | | | | | | | | | | | |
| 2011 | 12 | 9 | 17 | 9 | 8 | 2 | 2 | | 2 | 1 | 1 | | | | 2011 | 12 |
| 2012 | 13 | 10 | 17 | 8 | 9 | 3 | 3 | | 3 | 2 | 1 | | | | 2012 | 13 |
| 2013 | 13 | 11 | 19 | 10 | 9 | 3 | 2 | 1 | 2 | 1 | 1 | | | | 2013 | 13 |
| 2014 | 12 | 9 | 15 | 8 | 7 | 4 | 3 | 1 | 2 | 1 | 1 | | | | 2014 | 12 |
| 2015 | 15 | 9 | 17 | 10 | 7 | 4 | 3 | 1 | 3 | 2 | 1 | | | | 2015 | 15 |
| Total | 65 | 48 | 85 | 45 | 40 | 16 | 13 | 3 | 12 | 7 | 5 | 0 | 0 | 0 | Total | 65 |
| | | | | | | | | | | | | | | | |
| 2016 | 11 | 12 | 13 | 4 | 9 | 4 | 1 | 3 | 5 | 5 | | 1 | 1 | | 2016 | 11 |
| 2017 | 15 | 9 | 16 | 11 | 5 | 6 | 2 | 4 | 2 | 2 | | | | | 2017 | 15 |

| Year | Men | Women | White | Men | Women | Black | Men | Women | Asian | Men | Women | Native American | Men | Women | Year | Men | Women |
|---|---|---|---|---|---|---|---|---|---|---|---|---|---|---|---|---|---|
| 2018 | 10 | 15 | 16 | 5 | 11 | 5 | 3 | 2 | 3 | 2 | 1 | 1 | | 1 | 2018 | 10 | 15 |
| Total | 36 | 36 | 45 | 20 | 25 | 15 | 6 | 9 | 10 | 9 | 1 | 2 | 1 | 1 | Total | 36 | 36 |
| | | | | | | | | | | | | | | | | | |
| Overall | | | | | | | | | | | | | | | Overall | | |
| Total | 637 | 377 | 815 | 520 | 295 | 127 | 73 | 54 | 60 | 40 | 20 | 4 | | 8 | Total | 637 | 377 |
| | | | | | | | | | | | | | | | | | |
| Year | Men | Women | White | Men | Women | Black | Men | Women | Asian | Men | Women | Native American | Men | Women | Year | Men | Women |
| 1981 | 35 | 6 | 36 | 32 | 4 | 4 | 3 | 1 | | | | 1 | | 1 | 1981 | 35 | 6 |
| 1982 | 17 | 1 | 15 | 14 | 1 | 1 | 1 | | 1 | 1 | | 1 | 1 | | 1982 | 17 | 1 |
| 1983 | 28 | 6 | 33 | 27 | 6 | | | | 1 | 1 | | | | | 1983 | 28 | 6 |
| 1984 | 39 | 7 | 44 | 39 | 5 | 2 | | 2 | | | | | | | 1984 | 39 | 7 |
| 1985 | 21 | 4 | 22 | 20 | 2 | 2 | | | 2 | 1 | 1 | | | | 1985 | 21 | 4 |
| Total | 140 | 24 | 150 | 132 | 18 | 9 | 4 | 5 | 3 | 3 | 0 | 2 | 1 | 1 | Total | 140 | 24 |
| | | | | | | | | | | | | | | | | | |
| 1986 | 23 | 2 | 24 | 22 | 2 | 1 | 1 | | | | | | | | 1986 | 23 | 2 |
| 1987 | 28 | 4 | 28 | 25 | 3 | 2 | 1 | 1 | 1 | 1 | | 1 | 1 | | 1987 | 28 | 4 |
| 1988 | 23 | 6 | 25 | 19 | 6 | 4 | 4 | | | | | | | | 1988 | 23 | 6 |
| 1989 | 20 | 9 | 25 | 18 | 7 | 4 | 2 | 2 | | | | | | | 1989 | 20 | 9 |
| 1990 | 23 | 13 | 31 | 19 | 12 | 5 | 4 | 1 | | | | | | | 1990 | 23 | 13 |
| Total | 117 | 34 | 133 | 103 | 30 | 16 | 12 | 4 | 1 | 1 | 0 | 1 | 1 | 0 | Total | 117 | 34 |
| | | | | | | | | | | | | | | | | | |
| 1991 | 22 | 9 | 25 | 18 | 7 | 4 | 3 | 1 | 1 | 1 | | 1 | | 1 | 1991 | 22 | 9 |
| 1992 | 17 | 17 | 31 | 16 | 15 | 3 | 1 | 2 | | | | | | | 1992 | 17 | 17 |
| 1993 | 18 | 13 | 24 | 12 | 12 | 6 | 5 | 1 | 1 | 1 | | | | | 1993 | 18 | 13 |
| 1994 | 14 | 7 | | 9 | 6 | | 4 | | | 1 | | | | 1 | 1994 | 14 | 7 |
| 1995 | 9 | 15 | 20 | 7 | 13 | 2 | 2 | 2 | | | | | | | 1995 | 9 | 15 |
| Total | 80 | 61 | 100 | 62 | 53 | 15 | 15 | 6 | 2 | 3 | 0 | 1 | 0 | 2 | Total | 80 | 61 |
| | | | | | | | | | | | | | | | | | |
| 1996 | 13 | 8 | 14 | 10 | 4 | 5 | 2 | 3 | 2 | 1 | 1 | | | | 1996 | 13 | 8 |
| 1997 | 13 | 10 | 19 | 11 | 8 | 2 | 1 | 1 | 1 | 1 | | 1 | | 1 | 1997 | 13 | 10 |
| 1998 | 19 | 12 | 26 | 15 | 11 | 2 | 2 | | 3 | 2 | 1 | | | | 1998 | 19 | 12 |
| 1999 | 17 | 15 | 26 | 13 | 13 | 4 | 3 | 1 | 1 | 1 | | 1 | | 1 | 1999 | 17 | 15 |
| 2000 | 13 | 13 | 21 | 11 | 10 | 3 | | 3 | 2 | 2 | | | | | 2000 | 13 | 13 |
| Total | 75 | 58 | 106 | 60 | 46 | 16 | 8 | 8 | 9 | 7 | 2 | 2 | 0 | 2 | Total | 75 | 58 |

| Year | Men | Women | White | Men | Women | Black | Men | Women | Asian | Men | Women | Native American | Men | Women | Year | Men | Women |
|---|---|---|---|---|---|---|---|---|---|---|---|---|---|---|---|---|---|
| 2001 | 12 | 11 | 18 | 10 | 8 | 2 |  | 2 | 3 | 2 | 1 |  |  |  | 2001 | 12 | 11 |
| 2002 | 14 | 10 | 20 | 10 | 10 | 3 | 3 |  | 1 | 1 |  |  |  |  | 2002 | 14 | 10 |
| 2003 | 12 | 12 | 17 | 11 | 6 | 4 |  | 4 | 3 | 1 | 2 |  |  |  | 2003 | 12 | 12 |
| 2004 | 10 | 13 | 17 | 6 | 11 | 4 | 3 | 1 | 1 | 1 |  | 1 |  |  | 1 | 2004 | 10 | 13 |
| 2005 | 14 | 11 | 20 | 13 | 7 | 4 | 1 | 3 | 1 |  | 1 |  |  |  | 2005 | 14 | 11 |
| Total | 62 | 57 | 92 | 50 | 42 | 17 | 7 | 10 | 9 | 5 | 4 | 1 | 0 | 1 | Total | 62 | 57 |
| 2006 | 14 | 11 | 19 | 11 | 8 | 3 | 1 | 2 | 3 | 2 | 1 |  |  |  | 2006 | 14 | 11 |
| 2007 | 13 | 11 | 15 | 9 | 6 | 4 | 2 | 2 | 4 | 1 | 3 | 1 | 1 |  | 2007 | 13 | 11 |
| 2008 | 11 | 14 | 20 | 9 | 11 | 5 | 2 | 3 |  |  |  |  |  |  | 2008 | 11 | 14 |
| 2009 | 12 | 12 | 19 | 9 | 10 | 2 | 1 | 1 | 3 | 2 | 1 |  |  |  | 2009 | 12 | 12 |
| 2010 | 12 | 11 | 16 | 10 | 6 | 3 | 2 | 1 | 3 |  | 3 | 1 |  | 1 | 2010 | 12 | 11 |
| Total | 62 | 59 | 89 | 48 | 41 | 17 | 8 | 9 | 13 | 5 | 8 | 2 | 1 | 1 | Total | 62 | 59 |
| 2011 | 12 | 9 | 17 | 9 | 8 | 2 | 2 |  | 2 | 1 | 1 |  |  |  | 2011 | 12 | 9 |
| 2012 | 13 | 10 | 17 | 8 | 9 | 3 | 3 |  | 3 | 2 | 1 |  |  |  | 2012 | 13 | 10 |
| 2013 | 13 | 11 | 19 | 10 | 9 | 3 | 2 | 1 | 2 | 1 | 1 |  |  |  | 2013 | 13 | 11 |
| 2014 | 12 | 9 | 15 | 8 | 7 | 4 | 3 | 1 | 2 | 1 | 1 |  |  |  | 2014 | 12 | 9 |
| 2015 | 15 | 9 | 17 | 10 | 7 | 4 | 3 | 1 | 3 | 2 | 1 |  |  |  | 2015 | 15 | 9 |
| Total | 65 | 48 | 85 | 45 | 40 | 16 | 13 | 3 | 12 | 7 | 5 | 0 | 0 | 0 | Total | 65 | 48 |
| 2016 | 11 | 12 | 13 | 4 | 9 | 4 | 1 | 3 | 5 | 5 |  | 1 | 1 |  | 2016 | 11 | 12 |
| 2017 | 15 | 9 | 16 | 11 | 5 | 6 | 2 | 4 | 2 | 2 |  |  |  |  | 2017 | 15 | 9 |
| 2018 | 10 | 15 | 16 | 5 | 11 | 5 | 3 | 2 | 3 | 2 | 1 | 1 |  | 1 | 2018 | 10 | 15 |
| Total | 36 | 36 | 45 | 20 | 25 | 15 | 6 | 9 | 10 | 9 | 1 | 2 | 1 | 1 | Total | 36 | 36 |
| Overall Total | 637 | 377 | 815 | 520 | 295 | 127 | 73 | 54 | 60 | 40 | 20 | 4 |  | 8 | Overall Total | 637 | 377 |
| Year | Men | Women | White | Men | Women | Black | Men | Women | Asian | Men | Women | Native American | Men | Women | Year | Men | Women |
| 1981 | 35 | 6 | 36 | 32 | 4 | 4 | 3 | 1 |  |  | 1 |  | 1 | 1981 | 35 | 6 |

| 1982 | 17 | 1 | 15 | 14 | 1 | 1 | 1 |  | 1 | 1 |  | 1 | 1 |  |  | 1982 | 17 | 1 |
|---|---|---|---|---|---|---|---|---|---|---|---|---|---|---|---|---|---|---|
| 1983 | 28 | 6 | 33 | 27 | 6 |  |  |  | 1 | 1 |  |  |  |  |  | 1983 | 28 | 6 |
| 1984 | 39 | 7 | 44 | 39 | 5 | 2 |  | 2 |  |  |  |  |  |  |  | 1984 | 39 | 7 |
| 1985 | 21 | 4 | 22 | 20 | 2 | 2 |  | 2 | 1 | 1 |  |  |  |  |  | 1985 | 21 | 4 |
| Total | 140 | 24 | 150 | 132 | 18 | 9 | 4 | 5 | 3 | 3 | 0 | 2 | 1 |  | 1 | Total | 140 | 24 |
|  |  |  |  |  |  |  |  |  |  |  |  |  |  |  |  |  |  |  |
| 1986 | 23 | 2 | 24 | 22 | 2 | 1 | 1 |  |  |  |  |  |  |  |  | 1986 | 23 | 2 |
| 1987 | 28 | 4 | 28 | 25 | 3 | 2 | 1 | 1 | 1 | 1 |  | 1 |  |  | 1 | 1987 | 28 | 4 |
| 1988 | 23 | 6 | 25 | 19 | 6 | 4 | 4 |  |  |  |  |  |  |  |  | 1988 | 23 | 6 |
| 1989 | 20 | 9 | 25 | 18 | 7 | 4 | 2 | 2 |  |  |  |  |  |  |  | 1989 | 20 | 9 |
| 1990 | 23 | 13 | 31 | 19 | 12 | 5 | 4 | 1 |  |  |  |  |  |  |  | 1990 | 23 | 13 |
| Total | 117 | 34 | 133 | 103 | 30 | 16 | 12 | 4 | 1 | 1 | 0 | 1 | 1 |  | 0 | Total | 117 | 34 |
|  |  |  |  |  |  |  |  |  |  |  |  |  |  |  |  |  |  |  |
| 1991 | 22 | 9 | 25 | 18 | 7 | 4 | 3 | 1 | 1 | 1 |  | 1 |  |  | 1 | 1991 | 22 | 9 |
| 1992 | 17 | 17 | 31 | 16 | 15 | 3 | 1 | 2 |  |  |  |  |  |  |  | 1992 | 17 | 17 |
| 1993 | 18 | 13 | 24 | 12 | 12 | 6 | 5 | 1 | 1 | 1 |  |  |  |  |  | 1993 | 18 | 13 |
| 1994 | 14 | 7 |  | 9 | 6 |  | 4 |  |  | 1 |  |  |  |  | 1 | 1994 | 14 | 7 |
| 1995 | 9 | 15 | 20 | 7 | 13 | 2 | 2 | 2 |  |  |  |  |  |  |  | 1995 | 9 | 15 |
| Total | 80 | 61 | 100 | 62 | 53 | 15 | 15 | 6 | 2 | 3 | 0 | 1 | 0 |  | 2 | Total | 80 | 61 |
|  |  |  |  |  |  |  |  |  |  |  |  |  |  |  |  |  |  |  |
| 1996 | 13 | 8 | 14 | 10 | 4 | 5 | 2 | 3 | 2 | 1 | 1 |  |  |  |  | 1996 | 13 | 8 |
| 1997 | 13 | 10 | 19 | 11 | 8 | 2 | 1 | 1 | 1 | 1 |  | 1 |  |  | 1 | 1997 | 13 | 10 |
| 1998 | 19 | 12 | 26 | 15 | 11 | 2 | 2 |  | 3 | 2 | 1 |  |  |  |  | 1998 | 19 | 12 |
| 1999 | 17 | 15 | 26 | 13 | 13 | 4 | 3 | 1 | 1 | 1 |  | 1 |  |  | 1 | 1999 | 17 | 15 |
| 2000 | 13 | 13 | 21 | 11 | 10 | 3 |  | 3 | 2 | 2 |  |  |  |  |  | 2000 | 13 | 13 |
| Total | 75 | 58 | 106 | 60 | 46 | 16 | 8 | 8 | 9 | 7 | 2 | 2 | 0 |  | 2 | Total | 75 | 58 |

Source: Compiled and computed based on data provided by the MacArthur Fellows Program (June 2017 to February 2019) at: https://www.macfound.org/fellows/search/all.

## Earned Highest/Terminal Higher Education Degrees of MacArthur Fellows, 1981 to 2018, by Sex and Race

Table 7 presents data on the number of terminal or highest college degrees earned by MacArthur Fellows. Of the 1,014 Fellows, data for degrees are available for 928 (91.5%) Fellows, who earned a total of 965 terminal or highest college degrees. Thirty-seven Fellows earned two degrees each. Of the 637 male Fellows, 566 (88.9%) earned 593 terminal or highest college degrees: 468 (90%) out of 520 White men, earned 490 degrees; 58 (79.5%) out of 73 Black men, earned 60 degrees; 36 (90%) out of 40 Asian men, earned 39 degrees; and 4 Native American men earned 1 degree each. Of the 377 female Fellows, 362 (92%) earned 372 terminal or highest college degrees: 287 (97.3%) out of 295 White women, earned 293 degrees; 48 (88.9%) out of 54 Black women, earned 50 degrees; 19 (95%) out of 20 Asian women, earned 21 degrees; and all 8 Native American women earned 1 degree each. Of the 22 White male Fellows who earned 2 degrees each, 1 earned two bachelor's degrees (BA/BA); 6 earned two master's degrees each (6 M.A. degrees, 2 M.S. degrees, 1 M.ED., M.F.A., M.P.A., and M.B.A. each); 4 earned a JD; 5 earned an MD, and 21 earned a doctoral degree. Two Black men earned 2 bachelor's degrees each; and 3 Asian men earned 2 degrees each (1 earned 2 MA degrees, 1 earned an MD and a Ph.D., and 1 earned a PhD and a D.Sc.). Of the 6 White women who earned 2 degrees each, 1 earned 2 bachelor's degrees, 4 earned 2 master's degrees, and 1 earned a PhD. and an MD; 2 Black women earned 2 degrees each (1 earned 2 master's degrees and 1 earned 2 Ph.D.s), and 2 Asian women earned 2 master's degrees each.

According to Table 7, of the 965 terminal or highest college degrees earned by 928 Fellows, 540 (56%) are doctorates (351 by men and 189 by women), with 514 (53.3% of 965 total) being Ph.D.s.; 203 (21%) are master's degrees (106 by men and 97 by women), including 77 (8% of 965) M.A. degrees, 75 (7.8%% of 965) M.F.A.degrees, and 19 (2% of 965) M.S. degrees; 144 (15%) are bachelor's degrees (90 by men and 54 by women), including 92 (9.5% of 965) B.A. degrees, 15 (1.6% of 965) B.S. degrees, and 12 (1.2% of 965) B.F.A. degrees; 37 (3.8% of 965) M.D.s (27 by men and 10 by women); 36 (3.7% of 965) JDs (19 by women and 17 by men); 3 (0.3% of 965) Diplomas/Associate degrees (1 Black woman, 1 Native American woman, and 1 Black man); 1 (0.1%) Licenciatura degree (a White woman) and 1 (0.1%) C.Phil. degree (a White man).

Of the 965 total degrees earned, 490 (50.8%) are earned by White men; 293 (30.4%) are earned by White women; 60 (6.2%) are earned by Black men; 50 (5.2%) are earned by Black women; 39 (4%) are earned by Asian men; 21 (2.2%) are earned by Asian women; 8 (0.8%) are earned by Native American women, and 4 (0.4%) are earned by Native

American men. Of the 540 doctoral degrees earned, 310 (57.4%, but 32.1% of total) are earned by White men; 160 (29.6%, but 16.6% of total) are earned by White women; 14 (2.6%, but 1.5% total) each are earned by Black men and Black women; 25 (4.6%, but 2.6% of total) are earned by Asian men; 13 (2.4%, but 1.3% of total) are earned by Asian women, and 2 (0.4%, but 0.2% of total) each are earned by Native American men and Native American women. Of the 37 Doctor of Medicine (MD) degrees earned, 21 (56.8%) are earned by White men; 6 (16.2%) are earned by White women; 4 (10.8%) are earned by Black women; and 3 (8.1%) each are earned by Asian men and Black men. Of the 36 Juris Doctor (JD) degrees earned, 14 (38.9%) are earned by White women; 13 (36%) are earned by White men; 4 (11.1%) are earned by Black women; 2 (5.6%) each are earned by Asian men and Black men; and 1 (2.8%) is earned by an Asian woman. Of the 203 master's degrees earned, 75 (36.9%) are earned by White men; 71 (35%) are earned by White women; 23 (11.3%) are earned by Black men;17 (8.4%) are earned by Black women; 6 (3%) each are earned by Asian men and Asian women; 3 (1.5%) are earned by Native American women; and 2 (1%) are earned by Native American men. Of the 144 bachelor's degrees earned, 70 (48.6%) are earned by White men; 41 (28.5%) are earned by White women; 17 (11.8%) are earned by Black men; 10 (6.9%) are earned by Black women; 3 (2.1%) are earned by Asian men; 2 (1.4%) are earned by Native American women, and 1 (0.7%) is earned by an Asian woman (Table 7).

Table 7. Earned Highest/Terminal Higher Education Degrees of MacArthur Fellows, 1981 to 2018, by Sex and Race
Note: WM = White men; WW = White women; BM = Black men; BW = Black women; AM = Asian men; AW = Asian women; NAM = Native American men; NAW = Native American women

| Degree/Type | All | % Total | Men | % Total | Women | % Total | WM | WW | BM | BW | AM | AW | NAM | NAW |
|---|---|---|---|---|---|---|---|---|---|---|---|---|---|---|
| **Associate** | | | | | | | | | | | | | | |
| A.A. | 1 | 33.3 | | | 1 | 50 | | | | 1 | | | | |
| A.S. | 1 | 33.3 | | | 1 | 50 | | | | | | | | 1 |
| Diploma | 1 | 33.3 | 1 | 100 | | | | | 1 | | | | | |
| Total | 3 | 100 | 1 | 100 | 2 | 100 | | | 1 | 1 | | | | 1 |
| % of all Degrees | | | 0.1 | | 0.2 | | | | 0.1 | 0.1 | | 0.0 | | 0.1 |
| | | | | | | | | | | | | | | |
| **Bachelor** | | | | | | | | | | | | | | |
| A.B. | 8 | 5.6 | 5 | 3.5 | 3 | 2.1 | 5 | 2 | | 1 | | | | |

| Degree | n | % | n | % | n | % | n | % | n | n | n | n | n | n | n | n |
|---|---|---|---|---|---|---|---|---|---|---|---|---|---|---|---|---|
| B.A. | 92 | 63.9 | 54 | 37.5 | 38 | 26.4 | | | 42 | 30 | 10 | 5 | 2 | 1 | | 2 |
| B.Arch. | 4 | 2.8 | 3 | 2.1 | 1 | 0.7 | | | 3 | 1 | | | | | | |
| B.E.E. | 1 | 0.7 | 1 | 0.7 | | | | | 1 | | | | | | | |
| B.F.A. | 12 | 8.3 | 9 | 6.3 | 3 | 2.1 | | | 5 | 2 | 4 | 1 | | | | |
| B.M. | 4 | 2.8 | 2 | 1.4 | 2 | 1.4 | | | 1 | 1 | 1 | 1 | | | | |
| B.S. | 15 | 10.4 | 11 | 7.6 | 4 | 2.8 | | | 8 | 3 | 2 | 1 | 1 | | | |
| B.Sc. | 1 | 0.7 | 1 | 0.7 | | | | | 1 | | | | | | | |
| L.L.B. | 5 | 3.5 | 4 | 2.8 | 1 | 0.7 | | | 4 | | | 1 | | | | |
| B.Mus. | 1 | 0.7 | | | 1 | 0.7 | | | | 1 | | | | | | |
| B.Phil. | 1 | 0.7 | | | 1 | 0.7 | | | | 1 | | | | | | |
| **Total** | 144 | 100 | 90 | 62.6 | 54 | 37.6 | | | 70 | 41 | 17 | 10 | 3 | 1 | | 2 |
| % of all Degrees | 15 | | 9.3 | | 5.6 | | | | 7.3 | 4.2 | 1.8 | 1.0 | 0.3 | 0.1 | 0.0 | 0.2 |
| | | | | | | | | | | | | | | | | |
| Licenciatura | 1 | 100 | | | 1 | 100 | | | 1 | | | | | | | |
| % of all Degrees | 0.1 | | | | 0.1 | | | | 0.1 | | | | | | | |
| | | | | | | | | | | | | | | | | |
| **Master's** | | | | | | | | | | | | | | | | |
| A.M. | 1 | 0.5 | 1 | 0.5 | | | | | 1 | | | | | | | |
| M.Mus. | 1 | 0.5 | 1 | 0.5 | | | | | 1 | | | | | | | |
| M.A. | 77 | 37.9 | 48 | 23.6 | 29 | 14.3 | | | 38 | 25 | 5 | 4 | 4 | | 1 | |
| M.B.A. | 3 | 1.5 | 2 | 0.9 | 1 | 0.5 | | | 1 | | 1 | | | | | 1 |
| M.ED | 6 | 3 | 1 | 0.5 | 5 | 2.5 | | | 1 | 3 | | 2 | | | | |
| M.F.A. | 75 | 36.9 | 29 | 14.4 | 46 | 22.7 | | | 15 | 30 | 13 | 11 | 1 | 4 | | 1 |
| M.M. | 3 | 1.5 | 2 | 0.9 | 1 | 0.5 | | | | 1 | 1 | 1 | | | | |
| M.P.A. | 4 | 2 | 3 | 1.5 | 1 | 0.5 | | | 3 | 1 | | | | | | |
| M.P.H. | 1 | 0.5 | 1 | 0.5 | | | | | 1 | | | | | | | |
| M.R.P. | 1 | 0.5 | 1 | 0.5 | | | | | | | | | | 1 | | |
| M.S. | 19 | 9.4 | 13 | 6.4 | 6 | 3.0 | | | 12 | 4 | 1 | | 2 | | | |
| M.S.W. | 2 | 0.9 | 1 | 0.5 | 1 | 0.5 | | | 1 | 1 | | | | | | |
| M.Sc. | 2 | 0.9 | 1 | 0.5 | 1 | 0.5 | | | 1 | | | | | | | 1 |
| M.U.P. | 1 | 0.5 | 1 | 0.5 | | | | | | | 1 | | | | | |
| A.D.V. | 1 | 0.5 | 1 | 0.5 | | | | | 1 | | | | | | | |
| M.A.T. | 1 | 0.5 | | | 1 | 0.5 | | | | 1 | | | | | | |
| M.Arch. | 1 | 0.5 | | | 1 | 0.5 | | | | 1 | | | | | | |

| Degree | | | | | | | | | | | | | | |
|---|---|---|---|---|---|---|---|---|---|---|---|---|---|---|
| M.L.A. | 1 | 0.5 | | | 1 | 0.5 | | 1 | | | | | | |
| M.P.S. | 1 | 0.5 | | | 1 | 0.5 | | 1 | | | | | | |
| M.S.E. | 1 | 0.5 | | | 1 | 0.5 | | 1 | | | | | | |
| M.St. | 1 | 0.5 | | | 1 | 0.5 | | 1 | | | | | | |
| **Total** | 203 | 100 | 106 | 52 | 97 | 48 | 75 | 71 | 23 | 17 | 6 | 6 | 2 | 3 |
| % of all Degrees | 21 | | 11.0 | | 10.1 | | 7.8 | 7.4 | 2.4 | 1.8 | 0.6 | 0.6 | 0.2 | 0.3 |
| | | | | | | | | | | | | | | |
| C.Phil. | 1 | 100 | 1 | 100 | | | 1 | | | | | | | |
| % of all Degrees | 0.1 | | 0.1 | | | | 0.1 | | | | | | | |
| | | | | | | | | | | | | | | |
| J.D. | 36 | 100 | 17 | 47.2 | 19 | 52.8 | 13 | 14 | 2 | 4 | 2 | 1 | | |
| % of all degrees | 3.7 | | 1.8 | | 2.0 | | 1.3 | 1.5 | 0.2 | 0.4 | 0.2 | 0.1 | | |
| | | | | | | | | | | | | | | |
| M.D. | 37 | 100 | 27 | 73 | 10 | 27 | 21 | 6 | 3 | 4 | 3 | | | |
| % of all Degrees | 3.8 | | 2.8 | | 1.0 | | 2.2 | 0.6 | 0.3 | 0.4 | 0.3 | | | |
| | | | | | | | | | | | | | | |
| **Doctorate** | | | | | | | | | | | | | | |
| D.M.A. | 2 | 0.37 | 2 | 0.37 | | | 1 | | 1 | | | | | |
| D.Min. | 1 | 0.19 | 1 | 0.19 | | | | | 1 | | | | | |
| D.Mus. | 1 | 0.19 | 1 | 0.19 | | | 1 | | | | | | | |
| Doc. des Lettres | 1 | 0.19 | 1 | 0.19 | | | 1 | | | | | | | |
| Doctorat de Sociologie | 1 | 0.19 | 1 | 0.19 | | | 1 | | | | | | | |
| D. Sc. | 2 | 0.37 | 2 | 0.37 | | | 1 | | | | 1 | | | |
| D.P.H | 1 | 0.19 | 1 | 0.19 | | | 1 | | | | | | | |
| D.Phil. | 9 | 1.7 | 8 | 1.5 | 1 | 0.19 | 8 | 1 | | | | | | |
| PhD. | 514 | 95.2 | 331 | 61.3 | 183 | 33.9 | 293 | 157 | 12 | 12 | 24 | 13 | 2 | 1 |
| Kandidat Degree (PhD) | 1 | 0.19 | 1 | 0.19 | | | 1 | | | | | | | |
| Sc.D. | 1 | 0.19 | 1 | 0.19 | | | 1 | | | | | | | |
| Th.D. | 1 | 0.19 | 1 | 0.19 | | | 1 | | | | | | | |
| Ed.D. | 4 | 0.7 | | | 4 | 0.7 | | 2 | | 2 | | | | |
| D.Ed. | 1 | 0.19 | | | 1 | 0.19 | | | | | | | | 1 |
| **Total** | 540 | 100 | 351 | 65 | 189 | 35.0 | 310 | 160 | 14 | 14 | 25 | 13 | 2 | 2 |
| % of all Degrees | 56 | | 36.4 | | 19.6 | | 32.1 | 16.6 | 1.5 | 1.5 | 2.6 | 1.3 | 0.2 | 0.2 |
| | | | | | | | | | | | | | | |
| **All Degrees** | 965 | | 593 | 61.5 | 372 | 38.5 | 490 | 293 | 60 | 50 | 39 | 21 | 4 | 8 |

| Percent | | | | | | 50.8 | 30.4 | 6.2 | 5.2 | 4.0 | 2.2 | 0.4 | 0.8 |

Source: Compiled and computed based on data provided by the MacArthur Fellows Program (June 2017 to February 2019) at: https://www.macfound.org/fellows/search/all.

## Alma Mater of Highest/Terminal Higher Education Degrees and Types of Degrees Earned by MacArthur Fellows, 1981 to 2018, by Sex and Race

The alma mater or higher education institution where an individual earns their degree plays an important role in that person's success in the United States and the world. This is also the case when it comes to those selected for the MacArthur Fellows Program. This has also been observed in other studies focusing on prominent individuals from many walks of life (Kaba, 2012b, 2013ab, 2015, 2016, 2017a). The MacArthur Fellows Program conducted a study on the alma maters of its Fellows focusing on first degrees, especially bachelor's degrees. The study finds that from 1981 to 2014, the MacArthur Fellows Program selected 918 Fellows, who attended 315 diverse higher education institutions. Of the 918 Fellows, 34% attended private research universities; 23% attended public universities; 14% attended private liberal arts colleges; 11% or 100 did not earn an undergraduate degree; 10% attended international higher education institutions; 4% attended private master's level and/or professional focused institutions; 3% attended special focus institutions, and 1% attended community/two-year institutions. There were 44 (4.8%) Fellows who attended women's colleges and universities, 40 (4.4%) Fellows attended religiously affiliated universities, and 15 (1.6%) Fellows attended historically Black colleges and universities or tribal colleges. Of the 100 Fellows that did not earn an undergraduate degree, 39 attended college but did not complete their program of study, 37 did not participate in higher education studies, and 24 did not complete their undergraduate degrees but hold advanced graduate degrees (Conrad, 2017).

The information on the state and region in the United States, country, and world region where a Fellow's alma matter is located is also very important because these entities tend to compete for talent (Kaba, 2012b, 2013ab, 2015, 2016, 2017a). This current study focuses on the terminal or highest degrees of MacArthur Fellows, including the state and region in the United States where the institution is located, the country outside the United States where the institution is located, and the world region where the country is located.

According to Table 8, of the 965 terminal or highest degrees earned by MacArthur Fellows from 1981 to 2018, 865 (89.6%) are earned from 232 institutions in the United States (174 institutions or 75%), and 100 degrees (10.4%) are earned from 58 (25%) institutions outside of the United States. Of the 865 degrees earned in the United States, 516 (59.7%) are earned by men, and 349 (40.3%) are earned by women: 424 (49%, but 43.94% of 965 total) are White men; 275 (31.8%, but 28.5% of total) are White women; 55 (6.4%, but 5.7% of total) are Black men; 47 (5.4%, but 4.9% of total) are Black women; 33 (3.8%, but 3.4% of total) are Asian men; 19 (2.2%, but 2% of total) are Asian women; 8 (0.92%, 0.83% of total) are Native American women; and 4 (0.5%, but 0.4% of total) are Native American men.

Of the 865 degrees earned in the United States, 475 (54.9%, but 49.2% of 965 total) are earned at institutions in the Northeast (280 by men and 195 by women); 187 (21.6%, but 19.4% of total) degrees are earned in the West (120 men and 67 women);115 (13.3%, but 11.9% of total) degrees are earned in the Midwest (70 men and 45 women); and 88 (10.2%, but 9.1% of total) degrees are earned in the South (46 by men and 42 by women).

Of the 475 degrees earned in the Northeast, 228 (48%, but 26.4% of U.S. total) are earned by White men; 156 (32.8%, but 18% of U.S. total) are earned by White women; 33 (6.9%, but 3.8% of U.S. total) are earned by Black men; 27 (5.7%, but 3.1% of U.S. total) are earned by Black women; 17 (3.6%, but 2% of total) are earned by Asian men; 11 (2.3%, but 1.3% of U.S. total) are earned by Asian women; 2 (0.4%, but 0.2% of U.S. total) are earned by Native American men and 1(0.2%, but 0.1% of total) is earned by a Native American woman. Of the 187 degrees earned in the West, 98 (52.4%, but 11.3% of U.S. total) are earned by White men; 52 (27.8%, but 6% of U.S. total) are earned by White women; 11 (5.9%, but 1.3% of U.S. total) are earned by Black men; 4 (2.1%, but 0.46% of U.S. total) are earned by Black women; 10 (5.4%, but 1.2% of U.S. total) are earned by Asian men; 5 (2.7%, 0.6% of U.S. total) are earned by Asian women; 6 (3.2%, but 0.7% of U.S. total) are earned by Native American women, and 1 (0.5%, but 0.12% of U.S. total) is earned by a Native American man.

Of the 115 degrees earned in the Midwest, 59 (51.3%, but 6.8% of U.S. total) are earned by White men; 36 (31.3%, but 4.2% of U.S. total) are earned by White women; 6 (5.2%, but 0.7% of U.S. total) are earned by Black women; 5 (4.3%, but 0.6% of U.S. total) each are earned by Asian men and Black men; 3 (2.6%, but 0.4% of U.S. total) are earned by Asian women; and 1 (0.9%, but 0.12% of U.S. total) is earned by a Native American man. Of the 88 degrees earned in the South, 39 (44.3%, but 4.5% of U.S. total) are earned by White men; 31 (35.2%, but 3.6% of U.S. total) are earned by White women; 10 (11.4%, but 1.2% of U.S. total) are earned by Black women; 6 (6.8%, but 0.7% of U.S. total) are earned by Black men, and 1 (2.3%, but 0.12% of U.S. total) each is earned by an Asian man and a Native American woman.

Examining the top 10 states that awarded the most degrees, the state of Massachusetts awarded the most number of degrees (176) from 17 institutions (107 degrees earned by men and 69 degrees earned by women); California awarded 155 degrees from 22 institutions (103 degrees earned by men and 52 degrees earned by women. New York state awarded 139 degrees from 32 institutions (76 degrees earned by men and 63 degrees earned by women); Connecticut awarded 66 degrees by 3 institutions (39 degrees earned by men and 27 degrees earned by women); New Jersey awarded 48 degrees by 4 institutions (33 degrees earned by men and 15 degrees earned by women); Illinois awarded 41 degrees by 6 institutions (31 degrees earned by men and 10 degrees earned by women); Maryland awarded 24 degrees by 3 institutions (13 degrees earned by women and 11 degrees earned by men); Michigan awarded 18 degrees by 5 institutions (9 degrees each earned by men and women); Pennsylvania awarded 23 degrees by 7 institutions (16 degrees earned by men and 7 degrees earned by women); Rhode Island awarded 16 degrees by 2 institutions (10 degrees earned by women and 6 degrees earned by men).

The following institutions awarded 10 or more degrees: Harvard University,119 degrees (13.8% of U.S. total, but 12.3% of all degrees); Yale University, 61 degrees (7.1% of U.S. total, but 6.3% of all degrees); University of California, Berkeley, 51 degrees (5.9% of U.S. total, but 5.3% of all degrees); Columbia University, 44 degrees (5.1% of U.S. total, but 4.6^% of all degrees); Princeton University, 41 degrees (4.7% of U.S. total, but 4.2% of all degrees); Massachusetts Institute of Technology, 32 degrees (3.7% of U.S. total, but 3.3% of all degrees); University of Chicago, 24 degrees (2.8% of U.S. total, but 2.5% of all degrees); California Institute of Technology, Cornell University, and Stanford University, each 20 degrees (2.3% of U.S. total, but 2.1% of all degrees);

New York University, 19 degrees (2.2% of U.S. total, but 2% of all degrees); University of California, Los Angeles, 17 degrees (1.97% of U.S. total, but 1.76% of all degrees); Johns Hopkins University, 16 degrees (1.85% of U.S. total, but 1.66% of all degrees); University of Michigan, 14 degrees (1.6% of U.S. total, but 1.5% of all degrees); City University of New York , the University of Iowa, the University of Pennsylvania, and the University of Washington, each awarded 12 degrees (1.4% of U.S. total, but 1.2% of all degrees); University of Wisconsin, Madison, 11 degrees (1.3% of U.S. total, but 1.1% of all degrees); and the University of California, San Francisco, 10 degrees (1.2% of U.S. total, but 1% of all degrees).

Of the 100 degrees awarded to Fellows at institutions outside of the United States, 78 (78%) are earned from 37 institutions in Europe (63 degrees earned by men and 15 degrees earned by women); 18 degrees earned at 17 institutions in Western Europe (16 by men and 2 by women); 48 degrees earned at 11 institutions in Northern Europe (35 by men and 13 by women); 11 degrees earned at 8 institutions in Northern Europe (all 11 are men); and 1 degree earned in Southern Europe. There are 7 degrees earned at 7 institutions in Asia (5 men and 2 women); 4 degrees earned in Eastern Asia (3 men and 1 woman); and 3 degrees earned in Western Asia (2 men and 1 woman). There are 5 degrees earned at 5 institutions in Latin America and the Caribbean (3 men and 2 women); 2 degrees earned in the Caribbean (2 men); 2 degrees earned in South America (1 man and 1 woman); and 1 degree earned by a woman in Central America. There are 3 degrees earned in Oceania (Australia, all men). 2 women earned a degree each in Africa (Egypt and Nigeria) (Table 8).

Table 8. Alma Mater of Earned Highest/Terminal Higher Education Degrees and type of Degrees of MacArthur Fellows, 1981 to 2018, by Sex and Race
N=232 institutions (174 institutions in the U.S. and 58 outside the U.S.)
Note: WM = White men; WW = White women; BM = Black men; BW = Black women; AM = Asian men; AW = Asian women; NAM = Native American men; NAW = Native American women

| Alma Mater | # | % of U.S. | % of all Fellows | Men | % | Women | % | WM | WW | BM | BW | AM | AW | NAM | NAW |
|---|---|---|---|---|---|---|---|---|---|---|---|---|---|---|---|
| Northeast | | | | | | | | | | | | | | | |
| Connecticut | | | | | | | | | | | | | | | |
| University of Connecticut | 2 | 0.2 | 0.2 | 2 | 100 | | | 1 | | | | 1 | | | |
| Wesleyan University | 3 | 0.3 | 0.3 | 3 | 100 | | | 2 | | | | 1 | | | |
| Yale University | 61 | 7.1 | 6.3 | 34 | 55.7 | 27 | 44.3 | 27 | 17 | 5 | 8 | 2 | 2 | | |

| | | | | | | | | | | | | | |
|---|---|---|---|---|---|---|---|---|---|---|---|---|---|
| Total | 66 | 7.6 | 6.8 | 39 | | 27 | | 30 | 17 | 5 | 8 | 4 | 2 | |
| | | | | | | | | | | | | | | |
| **Maine** | | | | | | | | | | | | | | |
| Bates College | 1 | 0.1 | 0.1 | 1 | 100 | | | | | 1 | | | | |
| University of Maine | 1 | 0.1 | 0.1 | 1 | 100 | | | 1 | | | | | | |
| Total | 2 | 0.2 | 0.2 | 2 | | | | 1 | | 1 | | | | |
| | | | | | | | | | | | | | | |
| **Massachusetts** | | | | | | | | | | | | | | |
| Amherst College | 1 | 0.1 | 0.1 | | | 1 | 100 | | 1 | | | | | |
| Boston College | 1 | 0.1 | 0.1 | | | 1 | 100 | | 1 | | | | | |
| Boston University | 1 | 0.1 | 0.1 | | | 1 | 100 | | | | 1 | | | |
| Brandeis University | 4 | 0.5 | 0.4 | 3 | 75 | 1 | 25 | 2 | 1 | 1 | | | | |
| Clark University | 1 | 0.1 | 0.1 | 1 | 100 | | | 1 | | | | | | |
| Hampshire College | 1 | 0.1 | 0.1 | 1 | 100 | | | 1 | | | | | | |
| Harvard University | 119 | 13.8 | 12.3 | 79 | 66.4 | 40 | 33.6 | 65 | 29 | 5 | 9 | 8 | 2 | 1 |
| Lesley University | 1 | 0.1 | 0.1 | | | 1 | 100 | | 1 | | | | | |
| Massachusetts Institute of Technology | 32 | 3.7 | 3.3 | 19 | 59.4 | 13 | 40.6 | 17 | 10 | 1 | | 1 | 2 | | 1 |
| Mount Holyoke College | 1 | 0.1 | 0.1 | | | 1 | 100 | | | | 1 | | | |
| New England Conservatory of Music | 1 | 0.1 | 0.1 | 1 | 100 | | | | | 1 | | | | |
| Northeastern University | 2 | 0.2 | 0.2 | | | 2 | 100 | | 2 | | | | | |
| Radcliffe College | 4 | 0.5 | 0.4 | | | 4 | 100 | | 3 | | 1 | | | |
| Smith College | 1 | 0.1 | 0.1 | | | 1 | 100 | | 1 | | | | | |
| Tufts University | 1 | 0.1 | 0.1 | 1 | 100 | | | 1 | | | | | | |
| University of Massachusetts, Amherst. | 4 | 0.5 | 0.4 | 1 | 25 | 3 | 75 | | 3 | | | | 1 | |
| Williams College | 1 | 0.1 | 0.1 | 1 | 100 | | | 1 | | | | | | |
| Total | 176 | 20.3 | 18.2 | 107 | | 69 | | 88 | 52 | 8 | 12 | 9 | 4 | 2 | 1 |

| Institution | | | | | | | | | | | | |
|---|---|---|---|---|---|---|---|---|---|---|---|---|
| **New Hampshire** | | | | | | | | | | | | |
| Dartmouth College | 2 | 0.2 | 0.2 | 1 | 50 | 1 | 50 | 1 | 1 | | | |
| University of New Hampshire | 2 | 0.2 | 0.2 | | | 2 | 100 | | 1 | | 1 | |
| Total | 4 | 0.5 | 0.4 | 1 | | 3 | | 1 | 2 | | 1 | |
| | | | | | | | | | | | | |
| **New Jersey** | | | | | | | | | | | | |
| Drew University | 1 | 0.1 | 0.1 | 1 | 100 | | | | 1 | | | |
| Princeton University | 41 | 4.7 | 4.2 | 27 | 65.9 | 14 | 34.1 | 24 | 14 | | 3 | |
| Rutgers University, New Brunswick | 5 | 0.6 | 0.5 | 4 | 80 | 1 | 20 | 3 | 1 | 1 | | |
| University of Medicine & Dentistry of New Jersey | 1 | 0.1 | 0.1 | 1 | 100 | | | 1 | | | | |
| Total | 48 | 5.5 | 5.0 | 33 | | 15 | | 28 | 15 | 2 | 3 | |
| | | | | | | | | | | | | |
| **New York** | | | | | | | | | | | | |
| Albany Medical College | 1 | 0.1 | 0.1 | | | 1 | 100 | 1 | | | | |
| Bank Street College of Education | 1 | 0.1 | 0.1 | | | 1 | 100 | | 1 | | | |
| Bard College | 1 | 0.1 | 0.1 | 1 | 100 | | | 1 | | | | |
| City Unity of New York | 12 | 1.4 | 1.2 | 4 | 33.3 | 8 | 66.7 | 3 | 7 | 1 | 1 | |
| Columbia University | 44 | 5.1 | 4.6 | 26 | 59.1 | 18 | 40.9 | 22 | 16 | 3 | 1 | 1 | 1 |
| Cooper Union School of Art | 2 | 0.2 | 0.2 | 1 | 50 | 1 | 50 | | 1 | 1 | | |
| Cornell University | 20 | 2.3 | 2.1 | 12 | 60 | 8 | 40 | 11 | 8 | 1 | | |
| Fordham University | 1 | 0.1 | 0.1 | 1 | 100 | | 0 | 1 | | | | |
| Hofstra University | 1 | 0.1 | 0.1 | | | 1 | 100 | | 1 | | | |
| Juilliard School | 4 | 0.5 | 0.4 | 2 | 50 | 2 | 50 | 2 | 2 | | | |
| Long Island University | 1 | 0.1 | 0.1 | 1 | 100 | | | 1 | | | | |
| Manhattan College | 1 | 0.1 | 0.1 | 1 | 100 | | | 1 | | | | |
| Manhattan School of Music | 3 | 0.3 | 0.3 | 2 | 66.7 | 1 | 33.3 | 1 | 1 | 1 | | |
| Mount St. Mary College | 1 | 0.1 | 0.1 | | | 1 | 100 | | 1 | | | |
| New School | 2 | 0.2 | 0.2 | | | 2 | 100 | | 2 | | | |
| New York Law School | 1 | 0.1 | 0.1 | 1 | 100 | | | 1 | | | | |
| New York University | 19 | 2.2 | 2.0 | 12 | 63.2 | 7 | 36.8 | 9 | 5 | 3 | 1 | 1 |

| Institution | | | | | | | | | | | | | |
|---|---|---|---|---|---|---|---|---|---|---|---|---|---|
| Rockefeller University | 3 | 0.3 | 0.3 | 2 | 66.7 | 1 | 33.3 | 2 | 1 | | | | |
| Sarah Lawrence College | 1 | 0.1 | 0.1 | | | 1 | 100 | | 1 | | | | |
| School of Visual Arts | 2 | 0.2 | 0.2 | | | 2 | 100 | | 2 | | | | |
| Siena College | 1 | 0.1 | 0.1 | 1 | 100 | | | 1 | | | | | |
| Skidmore College | 1 | 0.1 | 0.1 | | | 1 | 100 | | 1 | | | | |
| State University of New York, College of Environmental & Forestry | 1 | 0.1 | 0.1 | 1 | 100 | | | 1 | | | | | |
| State University of New York, Brockport | 1 | 0.1 | 0.1 | | | 1 | 100 | | 1 | | | | |
| State University of New York, Buffalo | 3 | 0.3 | 0.3 | | | 3 | 100 | | 2 | | 1 | | |
| State University of New York, Purchase | 1 | 0.1 | 0.1 | 1 | 100 | | | | 1 | | | | |
| State University of New York, Stony Brook | 1 | 0.1 | 0.1 | 1 | 100 | | | | 1 | | | | |
| Syracuse University | 4 | 0.5 | 0.4 | 2 | 50 | 2 | 50 | 2 | 1 | | 1 | | |
| Union College | 1 | 0.1 | 0.1 | | | 1 | 100 | | 1 | | | | |
| Union Theological Seminary | 1 | 0.1 | 0.1 | 1 | 100 | | | 1 | | | | | |
| University of Rochester | 2 | 0.2 | 0.2 | 2 | 100 | | | 2 | | | | | |
| Yeshiva University | 1 | 0.1 | 0.1 | 1 | 100 | | | 1 | | | | | |
| Total | 139 | 16.1 | 14.4 | 76 | | 63 | | 63 | 56 | 12 | 4 | 1 | 3 |
| **Pennsylvania** | | | | | | | | | | | | | |
| Bryn Mawr College | 1 | 0.1 | 0.1 | | | 1 | 100 | | 1 | | | | |
| Carnegie Mellon University | 2 | 0.2 | 0.2 | 2 | 100 | | | 2 | | | | | |
| Curtis Institute of Music | 1 | 0.1 | 0.1 | | | 1 | 100 | | 1 | | | | |
| Pennsylvania State University | 2 | 0.2 | 0.2 | 2 | 100 | | | 1 | | 1 | | | |
| Temple University | 2 | 0.2 | 0.2 | 2 | 100 | | | 2 | | | | | |
| University of Pennsylvania | 12 | 1.4 | 1.2 | 8 | 66.7 | 4 | 33.3 | 6 | 3 | 2 | | 1 | |
| University of Pittsburgh | 3 | 0.3 | 0.3 | 2 | 66.7 | 1 | 33.3 | | 1 | 2 | | | |
| Total | 23 | 2.7 | 2.4 | 16 | | 7 | | 11 | 6 | 5 | | 1 | |
| **Rhode Island** | | | | | | | | | | | | | |
| Brown University | 7 | 0.8 | 0.7 | 3 | 42.9 | 4 | 57.1 | 3 | 3 | | 1 | | |
| Rhode Island School of Design | 9 | 1.0 | 0.9 | 3 | 33.3 | 6 | 66.7 | 3 | 4 | | 1 | 1 | |

| | | | | | | | | | | | | | | |
|---|---|---|---|---|---|---|---|---|---|---|---|---|---|---|
| Total | 16 | 1.8 | 1.7 | 6 | | 10 | | 6 | 7 | | 2 | | 1 | |
| | | | | | | | | | | | | | | |
| **Vermont** | | | | | | | | | | | | | | |
| Goddard College | 1 | 0.1 | 0.1 | | | 1 | 100 | | 1 | | | | | |
| | | | | | | | | | | | | | | |
| Total | 475 | 54.9 | 49.2 | 280 | 58.9 | 195 | 41.1 | 228 | 156 | 33 | 27 | 17 | 11 | 2 | 1 |
| % of U.S. | | | | 32.4 | | 22.5 | | 26.4 | 18.0 | 3.8 | 3.1 | 2.0 | 1.3 | 0.2 | 0.1 |
| % of all Fellows | | | | 29.0 | | 20.2 | | 23.63 | 16.17 | 3.42 | 2.8 | 1.762 | 1.14 | 0.21 | 0.1 |
| | | | | | | | | | | | | | | |
| **Midwest** | | | | | | | | | | | | | | |
| **Illinois** | | | | | | | | | | | | | | |
| Loyola University Chicago | 1 | 0.1 | 0.1 | 1 | 100 | | | 0 | 1 | | | | | |
| Northwestern University | 5 | 0.6 | 0.5 | 2 | 40 | 3 | 60 | 2 | 3 | | | | | |
| School of the Art Institute of Chicago | 1 | 0.1 | 0.1 | 1 | 100 | | | 0 | 1 | | | | | |
| University of Chicago | 24 | 2.8 | 2.5 | 18 | 75 | 6 | 25 | 15 | 5 | 1 | | 1 | 1 | 1 | |
| University of Illinois, Urbana-Champaign | 9 | 1.0 | 0.9 | 9 | 100 | | | 7 | | | 2 | | | | |
| University of Illinois at Chicago Circle | 1 | 0.1 | 0.1 | | 0 | 1 | 100 | | 1 | | | | | |
| Total | 41 | 4.7 | 4.2 | 31 | | 10 | | 26 | 9 | 3 | | 1 | 1 | 1 | |
| **Indiana** | | | | | | | | | | | | | | |
| Indiana University | 7 | 0.8 | 0.7 | 6 | 85.7 | 1 | 14.3 | 5 | 1 | | | 1 | | | |
| Purdue University | 3 | 0.3 | 0.3 | 2 | 66.7 | 1 | 33.3 | | 1 | | | 2 | | | |
| Total | 10 | 1.2 | 1.0 | 8 | | 2 | | 5 | 2 | | | 3 | | | |
| | | | | | | | | | | | | | | |
| **Iowa** | | | | | | | | | | | | | | |
| University of Iowa | 12 | 1.4 | 1.2 | 5 | 41.7 | 7 | 58.3 | 5 | 5 | | | | 2 | | |
| Grinnell College | 1 | 0.1 | 0.1 | | 0 | 1 | 100 | | 1 | | | | | | |
| Total | 13 | 1.5 | 1.3 | 5 | | 8 | | 5 | 6 | | | | 2 | | |

| | | | | | | | | | | | | |
|---|---|---|---|---|---|---|---|---|---|---|---|---|
| Kansas | | | | | | | | | | | | |
| University of Kansas | 5 | 0.6 | 0.5 | 3 | 60 | 2 | 40 | 3 | 2 | | | |
| Total | | | | | | | | | | | | |
| | | | | | | | | | | | | |
| Michigan | | | | | | | | | | | | |
| Kalamazoo College | 1 | 0.1 | 0.1 | 1 | 100 | | 0 | 1 | | | | |
| Michigan State University | 1 | 0.1 | 0.1 | 1 | 100 | | 0 | | 1 | | | |
| Oakland University | 1 | 0.1 | 0.1 | | 0 | 1 | 100 | | 1 | | | |
| University of Michigan | 14 | 1.6 | 1.5 | 7 | 50 | 7 | 50 | 6 | 4 | 1 | 3 | |
| Western Michigan University | 1 | 0.1 | 0.1 | | 0 | 1 | 100 | | 1 | | | |
| Total | 18 | 2.1 | 1.9 | 9 | | 9 | | 7 | 5 | 2 | 4 | |
| | | | | | | | | | | | | |
| Minnesota | | | | | | | | | | | | |
| University of Minnesota | 4 | 0.5 | 0.4 | 1 | 25 | 3 | 75 | 1 | 2 | | 1 | |
| | | | | | | | | | | | | |
| Ohio | | | | | | | | | | | | |
| Antioch College | 2 | 0.2 | 0.2 | 1 | 50 | 1 | 50 | 1 | 1 | | | |
| Case Western Reserve University | 2 | 0.2 | 0.2 | 2 | 100 | | 0 | 2 | | | | |
| Oberlin College | 4 | 0.5 | 0.4 | 2 | 50 | 2 | 50 | 2 | 2 | | | |
| Oberlin Conservatory | 2 | 0.2 | 0.2 | | 0 | 2 | 100 | | 1 | 1 | | |
| Ohio State University | 1 | 0.1 | 0.1 | 1 | 100 | | 0 | 1 | | | | |
| Ohio University | 1 | 0.1 | 0.1 | 1 | 100 | | 0 | | | 1 | | |
| Total | 12 | 1.4 | 1.2 | 7 | | 5 | | 6 | 4 | 1 | 1 | |

| | | | | | | | | | | | | | |
|---|---|---|---|---|---|---|---|---|---|---|---|---|---|
| Wisconsin | | | | | | | | | | | | | |
| Milwaukee School of Engineering | 1 | 0.1 | 0.1 | 1 | 100 | | 0 | 1 | | | | | |
| University of Wisconsin, Madison | 11 | 1.3 | 1.1 | 5 | 45.5 | 6 | 54.5 | 5 | 6 | | | | |
| Total | 12 | 1.4 | 1.2 | 6 | | 6 | | 6 | 6 | | | | |
| | | | | | | | | | | | | | |
| Total | 115 | 13.3 | 11.9 | 70 | 60.87 | 45 | 39.13 | 59 | 36 | 5 | 6 | 5 | 3 | 1 |
| % of U.S. | | | | 8.1 | | 5.2 | | 6.821 | 4.162 | 0.58 | 0.69 | 0.578 | 0.35 | 0.12 |
| % of all Fellows | | | | 7.3 | | 4.7 | | 6.1 | 3.7 | 0.52 | 0.62 | 0.52 | 0.31 | 0.10 |
| | | | | | | | | | | | | | |
| South | | | | | | | | | | | | | |
| Alabama | | | | | | | | | | | | | |
| Auburn University | 2 | 0.231 | 0.21 | 1 | 50 | 1 | 50 | 1 | | 1 | | | |
| Samford University | 1 | 0.116 | 0.10 | | 0 | 1 | 100 | | | 1 | | | |
| University of Alabama, Birmingham | 1 | 0.116 | 0.10 | | 0 | 1 | 100 | | | 1 | | | |
| Total | 4 | 0.46 | 0.41 | 1 | | 3 | | 1 | | 3 | | | |
| | | | | | | | | | | | | | |
| Arkansas | | | | | | | | | | | | | |
| Philander Smith College | 1 | 0.116 | 0.10 | 1 | 100 | | 0 | | 1 | | | | |
| University of Arkansas | 1 | 0.116 | 0.10 | | 0 | 1 | 100 | 1 | | | | | |
| Total | 2 | 0.23 | 0.21 | 1 | | 1 | | 1 | 1 | | | | |
| | | | | | | | | | | | | | |
| Florida | | | | | | | | | | | | | |
| Florida International Seminary | 1 | 0.116 | 0.10 | 1 | 100 | | 0 | 1 | | | | | |
| University of Florida | 4 | 0.462 | 0.41 | 1 | 25 | 3 | 75 | 1 | 2 | 1 | | | |
| University of Miami | 1 | 0.116 | 0.10 | 1 | 100 | | 0 | | 1 | | | | |
| Total | 6 | 0.69 | 0.62 | 3 | | 3 | | 2 | 2 | 1 | 1 | | |

| Institution | | | | | | | | | | | | |
|---|---|---|---|---|---|---|---|---|---|---|---|---|
| Georgia | | | | | | | | | | | | |
| Emory University | 1 | 0.116 | 0.10 | | 0 | 1 | 100 | 1 | | | | |
| Georgia Institute of Technology | 1 | 0.116 | 0.10 | 1 | 100 | | 0 | | | | 1 | |
| University of Georgia | 2 | 0.231 | 0.21 | 2 | 100 | | 0 | 2 | | | | |
| Total | 4 | 0.46 | 0.41 | 3 | | 1 | | 2 | 1 | | 1 | |
| | | | | | | | | | | | | |
| Louisiana | | | | | | | | | | | | |
| Tulane University | 1 | 0.116 | 0.10 | 1 | 100 | | 0 | 1 | | | | |
| University of Louisiana at Lafayette | 1 | 0.116 | 0.10 | | 0 | 1 | 100 | | 1 | | | |
| University of Southwestern Louisiana | 1 | 0.116 | 0.10 | | 0 | 1 | 100 | | 1 | | | |
| Total | 3 | 0.35 | 0.31 | 1 | | 2 | | 1 | 2 | | | |
| | | | | | | | | | | | | |
| Maryland | | | | | | | | | | | | |
| Johns Hopkins University | 16 | 1.85 | 1.66 | 9 | 56.25 | 7 | 43.75 | 8 | 5 | 1 | 2 | |
| Maryland Institute College of Art | 1 | 0.116 | 0.10 | | 0 | 1 | 100 | | 1 | | | |
| University of Maryland, College Park | 7 | 0.809 | 0.73 | 2 | 28.6 | 5 | 71.4 | 2 | 5 | | | |
| Total | 24 | 2.77 | 2.49 | 11 | | 13 | | 10 | 11 | 1 | 2 | |
| | | | | | | | | | | | | |
| North Carolina | | | | | | | | | | | | |
| Duke University | 6 | 0.694 | 0.62 | 3 | 50 | 3 | 50 | 2 | 3 | 1 | | |
| North Carolina State University | 1 | 0.116 | 0.10 | 1 | 100 | | 0 | 1 | | | | |
| University of North Carolina, Chapel Hill | 4 | 0.462 | 0.41 | 1 | 25 | 3 | 75 | 1 | 1 | | 2 | |
| University of North Carolina at Greensboro | 1 | 0.116 | 0.10 | | 0 | 1 | 100 | | 1 | | | |
| Wake Forest College | 1 | 0.116 | 0.10 | 1 | 100 | | 0 | 1 | | | | |
| Total | 13 | 1.5 | 1.35 | 6 | | 7 | | 5 | 5 | 1 | 2 | |

| | | | | | | | | | | | | | |
|---|---|---|---|---|---|---|---|---|---|---|---|---|---|
| Oklahoma | | | | | | | | | | | | | |
| University of Tulsa | 1 | 0.116 | 0.10 | 1 | 100 | | 0 | 1 | | | | | |
| | | | | | | | | | | | | | |
| Tennessee | | | | | | | | | | | | | |
| Meharry Medical College | 1 | 0.116 | 0.10 | 1 | 100 | | 0 | | 1 | | | | |
| University of Tennessee | 1 | 0.116 | 0.10 | 1 | 100 | | 0 | 1 | | | | | |
| Vanderbilt University | 2 | 0.231 | 0.21 | 1 | 50 | 1 | 50 | 1 | 1 | | | | |
| Total | 4 | 0.462 | 0.41 | 3 | | 1 | | 2 | 1 | 1 | | | |
| | | | | | | | | | | | | | |
| Texas | | | | | | | | | | | | | |
| Texas A & M University | 1 | 0.116 | 0.10 | 1 | 100 | | 0 | 1 | | | | | |
| University of Houston | 1 | 0.116 | 0.10 | 1 | 100 | | 0 | 1 | | | | | |
| University of Texas at Austin | 8 | 0.925 | 0.83 | 6 | 75 | 2 | 25 | 6 | 2 | | | | |
| Total | 10 | 1.16 | 1.04 | 8 | | 2 | | 8 | 2 | | | | |
| | | | | | | | | | | | | | |
| Virginia | | | | | | | | | | | | | |
| George Mason University | 1 | 0.116 | 0.10 | | 0 | 1 | 100 | | | 1 | | | |
| Old Dominion University | 1 | 0.116 | 0.10 | | 0 | 1 | 100 | | | | | | 1 |
| University of Virginia | 5 | 0.578 | 0.52 | 3 | 60 | 2 | 40 | 2 | 2 | 1 | | | |
| Virginia Commonwealth University | 2 | 0.231 | 0.21 | | 0 | 2 | 100 | | 2 | | | | |
| Total | 9 | 1.04 | 0.93 | 3 | | 6 | | 2 | 4 | 1 | 1 | | 1 |
| | | | | | | | | | | | | | |
| Washington, D.C. | | | | | | | | | | | | | |
| American University | 2 | 0.231 | 0.21 | 2 | 100 | | 0 | 2 | | | | | |
| Catholic University | 1 | 0.116 | 0.10 | 1 | 100 | | 0 | 1 | | | | | |

| | | | | | | | | | | | | | | |
|---|---|---|---|---|---|---|---|---|---|---|---|---|---|---|
| Georgetown University | 1 | 0.116 | 0.10 | | 0 | 1 | 100 | | 1 | | | | | |
| George Washington University | 2 | 0.231 | 0.21 | 1 | 50 | 1 | 50 | 1 | 1 | | | | | |
| Howard University | 1 | 0.116 | 0.10 | | 0 | 1 | 100 | | | | 1 | | | |
| Total | 7 | 0.81 | 0.73 | 4 | | 3 | | 4 | 2 | | 1 | | | |
| | | | | | | | | | | | | | | |
| | | | | | | | | | | | | | | |
| | | | | | | | | | | | | | | |
| West Virginia | | | | | | | | | | | | | | |
| West Virginia University | 1 | 0.116 | 0.10 | 1 | 100 | | 0 | 1 | | | | | | |
| | | | | | | | | | | | | | | |
| | | | | | | | | | | | | | | |
| | | | | | | | | | | | | | | |
| Total | 88 | 10.17 | 9.12 | 46 | 52.273 | 42 | 47.73 | 39 | 31 | 6 | 10 | 1 | | 1 |
| % of U.S. | | | | 5.318 | | 4.86 | | 4.5 | 3.6 | 0.69 | 1.16 | 0.12 | | 0.12 |
| % of all Fellows | | | | 4.767 | | 4.4 | | 4.0 | 3.2 | 0.62 | 1.04 | 0.104 | | 0.10 |
| | | | | | | | | | | | | | | |
| West | | | | | | | | | | | | | | |
| Alaska | | | | | | | | | | | | | | |
| Alaska Pacific University | 1 | 0.116 | 0.10 | | 0 | 1 | 100 | | | | | | | 1 |
| | | | | | | | | | | | | | | |
| | | | | | | | | | | | | | | |
| Arizona | | | | | | | | | | | | | | |
| Arizona State University | 1 | 0.116 | 0.10 | 1 | 100 | | 0 | 1 | | | | | | |
| University of Arizona | 3 | 0.347 | 0.31 | 2 | 66.7 | 1 | 33.3 | 2 | | | | | | 1 |
| Total | 4 | 0.46 | 0.41 | 3 | | 1 | | 3 | | | | | | 1 |
| | | | | | | | | | | | | | | |
| | | | | | | | | | | | | | | |
| California | | | | | | | | | | | | | | |
| American Conservatory Theater | 1 | 0.116 | 0.10 | | 0 | 1 | 100 | | | | 1 | | | |
| Art Center College of Design | 1 | 0.116 | 0.10 | 1 | 100 | | 0 | 1 | | | | | | |
| California Institute of the Arts | 2 | 0.231 | 0.21 | 2 | 100 | | 0 | 1 | | 1 | | | | |

| Institution | | | | | | | | | | | | | |
|---|---|---|---|---|---|---|---|---|---|---|---|---|---|
| California Institute of Technology | 20 | 2.312 | 2.07 | 16 | 80 | 4 | 20 | 14 | 4 | 1 | | 1 | |
| California State University at East Bay | 1 | 0.116 | 0.10 | 1 | 100 | | 0 | | | | | 1 | |
| Claremont Graduate School | 3 | 0.347 | 0.31 | 1 | 33.3 | 2 | 66.7 | 1 | 2 | | | | |
| Mills College | 3 | 0.347 | 0.31 | | 0 | 3 | 100 | | 2 | | 1 | | |
| Otis Art Institute | 1 | 0.116 | 0.10 | 1 | 100 | | 0 | | 1 | | | | |
| Pasadena City College | 1 | 0.116 | 0.10 | | 0 | 1 | 100 | | | | 1 | | |
| Pepperdine University | 1 | 0.116 | 0.10 | 1 | 100 | | 0 | | 1 | | | | |
| San Francisco State College | 1 | 0.116 | 0.10 | 1 | 100 | | 0 | | 1 | | | | |
| Scripps Research Institute | 1 | 0.116 | 0.10 | 1 | 100 | | 0 | 1 | | | | | |
| Sonoma State University | 1 | 0.116 | 0.10 | 1 | 100 | | 0 | 1 | | | | | |
| Stanford University | 20 | 2.312 | 2.07 | 16 | 80 | 4 | 20 | 14 | 2 | | | 2 | 2 |
| University of California, Berkeley | 51 | 5.896 | 5.28 | 36 | 70.6 | 15 | 29.4 | 31 | 13 | 1 | | 4 | 2 |
| University of California, Los Angeles | 17 | 1.965 | 1.76 | 9 | 52.9 | 8 | 47.1 | 6 | 7 | 1 | | 2 | | 1 |
| University of California, San Diego | 6 | 0.694 | 0.62 | 3 | 50 | 3 | 50 | 3 | 2 | | 1 | | |
| University of California, San Francisco | 10 | 1.156 | 1.04 | 6 | 60 | 4 | 40 | 4 | 4 | 2 | | | |
| University of California, Santa Barbara | 6 | 0.694 | 0.62 | 2 | 33.3 | 4 | 66.7 | 2 | 4 | | | | |
| University of California, Santa Cruz | 2 | 0.231 | 0.21 | 2 | 100 | | 0 | 2 | | | | | |
| University of Southern California | 4 | 0.462 | 0.41 | 2 | 50 | 2 | 50 | 2 | 1 | | | 1 | |
| Wright Institute | 2 | 0.231 | 0.21 | 1 | 50 | 1 | 50 | | 1 | 1 | | | |
| Total | 155 | 17.9 | 16.06 | 103 | | 52 | | 83 | 42 | 10 | 4 | 10 | 5 | 1 |

Colorado

| Institution | | | | | | | | | | | | | |
|---|---|---|---|---|---|---|---|---|---|---|---|---|---|
| University of Colorado at Boulder | 1 | 0.116 | 0.10 | 1 | 100 | | 0 | 1 | | | | | |
| University of Denver | 1 | 0.116 | 0.10 | | 0 | 1 | 100 | | 1 | | | | |
| Total | 2 | 0.231 | 0.21 | 1 | | 1 | | 1 | 1 | | | | |

Hawaii

| Institution | | | | | | | | | | | | | |
|---|---|---|---|---|---|---|---|---|---|---|---|---|---|
| University of Hawaii at Mānoa | 1 | 0.116 | 0.10 | | 0 | 1 | 100 | | 1 | | | | |

| Institution | | | | | | | | | | | | |
|---|---|---|---|---|---|---|---|---|---|---|---|---|
| **Montana** | | | | | | | | | | | | |
| Great Falls Commercial College | 1 | 0.116 | 0.10 | | 0 | 1 | 100 | | | | | 1 |
| Montana State University | 1 | 0.116 | 0.10 | | 0 | 1 | 100 | | | | | 1 |
| University of Montana | 1 | 0.116 | 0.10 | 1 | 100 | | 0 | | | | 1 | |
| Total | 3 | 0.35 | 0.31 | 1 | | 2 | | | | | 1 | 2 |
| **New Mexico** | | | | | | | | | | | | |
| University of New Mexico | 1 | 0.116 | 0.10 | | 0 | 1 | 100 | | | | | 1 |
| **Oregon** | | | | | | | | | | | | |
| Oregon Health and Science University | 1 | 0.116 | 0.10 | | 0 | 1 | 100 | 1 | | | | |
| Oregon State University | 1 | 0.116 | 0.10 | | 0 | 1 | 100 | 1 | | | | |
| Reed College | 1 | 0.1 | 0.1 | 1 | 100 | | 0 | 1 | | | | |
| University of Oregon | 1 | 0.116 | 0.10 | | 0 | 1 | 100 | 1 | | | | |
| Total | 4 | 0.462 | 0.41 | 1 | | 3 | | 1 | 3 | | | |
| **Utah** | | | | | | | | | | | | |
| University of Utah | 1 | 0.116 | 0.10 | 1 | 100 | | 0 | 1 | | | | |
| Utah State University | 1 | 0.116 | 0.10 | | 0 | 1 | 100 | | 1 | | | |
| Total | 2 | 0.23 | 0.21 | 1 | | 1 | | 1 | 1 | | | |
| **Washington** | | | | | | | | | | | | |
| Washington State University | 2 | 0.231 | 0.21 | 2 | 100 | | 0 | 1 | | 1 | | |

| | | | | | | | | | | | | | |
|---|---|---|---|---|---|---|---|---|---|---|---|---|---|
| University of Washington | 12 | 1.387 | 1.24 | 8 | 66.7 | 4 | 33.3 | 8 | 4 | | | | |
| Total | 14 | 1.62 | 1.45 | 10 | | 4 | | 9 | 4 | 1 | | | |
| | | | | | | | | | | | | | |
| | | | | | | | | | | | | | |
| | | | | | | | | | | | | | |
| Total | 187 | 21.62 | 19.38 | 120 | 64.2 | 67 | 35.8 | 98 | 52 | 11 | 4 | 10 | 5 | 1 | 6 |
| % of U.S. | | | | 13.9 | | 7.7 | | 11.33 | 6.01 | 1.27 | 0.46 | 1.16 | 0.58 | 0.12 | 0.69 |
| % of all Fellows | | | | 12.4 | | 6.9 | | 10.16 | 5.4 | 1.14 | 0.41 | 1.04 | 0.52 | 0.1 | 0.62 |
| | | | | | | | | | | | | | |
| United States Total | 865 | | 89.8 | 516 | 59.7 | 349 | 40.3 | 424 | 275 | 55 | 47 | 33 | 19 | 4 | 8 |
| % of all Fellows | | | | 53.5 | | 36.2 | | 43.94 | 28.5 | 5.7 | 4.87 | 3.42 | 1.97 | 0.41 | 0.83 |
| | | | | | | | | | | | | | |
| Canada | | | | | | | | | | | | | | |
| McGill University | 2 | | 0.21 | 1 | 50 | 1 | 50 | 1 | 1 | | | | | |
| University of British Columbia | 1 | | 0.10 | 1 | 100 | | 0 | 1 | | | | | | |
| University of Waterloo | 1 | | 0.10 | 1 | 100 | | 0 | 1 | | | | | | |
| University of Toronto | 1 | | 0.10 | | 0 | 1 | 100 | | 1 | | | | | |
| Total | 5 | | 0.52 | 3 | 60 | 2 | 40 | 3 | 2 | | | | | |
| % of all Fellows | | | | 0.311 | | 0.21 | | 0.31 | 0.21 | | | | | |
| | | | | | | | | | | | | | |
| Northern America | 870 | | 90.2 | 519 | 59.66 | 351 | 40.3 | 427 | 277 | 55 | 47 | 33 | 19 | 4 | 8 |
| % of all Fellows | | | | 53.8 | | 36.4 | | 44.2 | 28.7 | 5.7 | 4.9 | 3.4 | 2.0 | 0.4 | 0.8 |
| | | | | | | | | | | | | | |
| Africa | | | | | | | | | | | | | | |
| | | | | | | | | | | | | | |
| Western Africa | | | | | | | | | | | | | | |
| | | | | | | | | | | | | | |
| Nigeria | | | | | | | | | | | | | | |
| University of Ibadan | 1 | | 0.1 | | | 1 | 100 | | | | 1 | | | |
| | | | | | | | | | | | | | |
| Northern Africa | | | | | | | | | | | | | | |
| | | | | | | | | | | | | | |
| Egypt | | | | | | | | | | | | | | |
| Cairo University | 1 | | 0.1 | | | 1 | 100 | 1 | | | | | | |
| | | | | | | | | | | | | | |
| Africa Total | 2 | | 0.2 | | | 2 | 100 | 1 | | | 1 | | | |
| % of all Fellows | | | | | | 0.2 | | 0.104 | | | 0.1 | | | |
| | | | | | | | | | | | | | |
| Asia | | | | | | | | | | | | | | |

| | | | | | | | | | | | | |
|---|---|---|---|---|---|---|---|---|---|---|---|---|
| Eastern Asia | | | | | | | | | | | | |
| China | | | | | | | | | | | | |
| Central Academy of Fine Art, Beijing | 1 | | 0.1 | 1 | 100 | | | | | | 1 | |
| Chinese University of Hong | 1 | | 0.1 | 1 | 100 | | | | | | 1 | |
| University of Science and Technology of China | 1 | | 0.1 | 1 | 100 | | | | | | 1 | |
| | | | | | | | | | | | | |
| Japan | | | | | | | | | | | | |
| Kyoto University | 1 | | 0.1 | | 0 | 1 | 100 | | | | | 1 |
| Total | 4 | | 0.4 | 3 | 75 | 1 | 25 | | | | 3 | 1 |
| | | | | | | | | | | | | |
| Western Asia | | | | | | | | | | | | |
| Georgia | | | | | | | | | | | | |
| Tbilisi State University | 1 | | 0.1 | 1 | 100 | | | 1 | | | | |
| | | | | | | | | | | | | |
| Israel | | | | | | | | | | | | |
| Weizmann Institute of Science | 1 | | 0.1 | 1 | 100 | | | 1 | | | | |
| Technion – Israel Institute of Technology | 1 | | 0.1 | | 0 | 1 | 100 | | 1 | | | |
| Total | 3 | | 0.3 | 2 | 66.667 | 1 | 33.33 | 2 | 1 | | | |
| | | | | | | | | | | | | |
| Asia Total | 7 | | 0.7 | 5 | 71.429 | 2 | 28.57 | 2 | 1 | | 3 | 1 |
| % of all Fellows | | | 0.52 | | 0.21 | | 0.2 | 0.104 | 0 | 0 | 0.311 | 0.1 |
| | | | | | | | | | | | | |
| Europe | | | | | | | | | | | | |
| Eastern Europe | | | | | | | | | | | | |
| Hungary | | | | | | | | | | | | |
| Hungarian Academy of Sciences | 1 | | 0.1 | 1 | 100 | | | 1 | | | | |
| Institute of Construction | 1 | | 0.1 | 1 | 100 | | | 1 | | | | |
| | | | | | | | | | | | | |
| Poland | | | | | | | | | | | | |
| Institute of Social Sciences | 1 | | 0.1 | 1 | 100 | | | 1 | | | | |
| National Theatrical | 2 | | 0.2 | 2 | 100 | | | 2 | | | | |

| | | | | | | | | | | | | | |
|---|---|---|---|---|---|---|---|---|---|---|---|---|---|
| Academy | | | | | | | | | | | | | |
| University of Warsaw | 1 | | 0.1 | 1 | 100 | | | 1 | | | | | |
| | | | | | | | | | | | | | |
| | | | | | | | | | | | | | |
| Russia | | | | | | | | | | | | | |
| L.D. Landau Institute of Theo. Physics | 1 | | 0.1 | 1 | 100 | | | 1 | | | | | |
| Moscow State University | 3 | | 0.3 | 3 | 100 | | | 3 | | | | | |
| | | | | | | | | | | | | | |
| Ukraine | | | | | | | | | | | | | |
| Ukrainian Academy of Sciences | 1 | | 0.1 | 1 | 100 | | | 1 | | | | | |
| | | | | | | | | | | | | | |
| Total | 11 | | 1.1 | 11 | 100 | | | 11 | | | | | |
| % of all Fellows | | | 1.1 | | | | | 1.1 | | | | | |
| | | | | | | | | | | | | | |
| Northern Europe | | | | | | | | | | | | | |
| Denmark | | | | | | | | | | | | | |
| University of Aarhus | 1 | | 0.1 | | | 1 | 100 | 1 | | | | | |
| | | | | | | | | | | | | | |
| Ireland | | | | | | | | | | | | | |
| Trinity College, University of Dublin | 1 | | 0.1 | 1 | 100 | | | 1 | | | | | |
| | | | | | | | | | | | | | |
| Sweden | | | | | | | | | | | | | |
| Lund University | 1 | | 0.1 | | | 1 | 100 | 1 | | | | | |
| | | | | | | | | | | | | | |
| United Kingdom | | | | | | | | | | | | | |
| University of Cambridge | 15 | | 1.6 | 11 | 73.3 | 4 | 26.7 | 8 | 2 | 1 | 1 | 2 | 1 |
| London School of Economics | 2 | | 0.2 | 2 | 100 | | | 1 | | 1 | | | |
| University of Oxford | 18 | | 1.9 | 14 | 77.8 | 4 | 22.2 | 12 | 4 | 1 | | 1 | |
| University of London | 5 | | 0.5 | 3 | 60 | 2 | 40 | 3 | 2 | | | | |
| University College, London | 2 | | 0.2 | 1 | 50 | 1 | 50 | 1 | 1 | | | | |
| University of Manchester | 1 | | 0.1 | 1 | 100 | | | 1 | | | | | |
| University of the Arts London | 1 | | 0.1 | 1 | 100 | | | 1 | | | | | |
| University of East Anglia | 1 | | 0.1 | 1 | 100 | | | 1 | | | | | |
| Total | 45 | | 4.7 | 34 | | 11 | | 28 | 9 | 3 | 1 | 3 | 1 |

| Institution | | | | | | | | | | | | | | |
|---|---|---|---|---|---|---|---|---|---|---|---|---|---|---|
| Total | 48 | | 5.0 | 35 | 72.9 | 13 | 27.1 | 29 | 11 | 3 | 1 | 3 | 1 | |
| % of all Fellows | | | | 3.6 | | 1.3 | | 3.0 | 1.1 | 0.3 | 0.1 | 0.3 | 0.1 | |
| | | | | | | | | | | | | | | |
| **Southern Europe** | | | | | | | | | | | | | | |
| Italy | | | | | | | | | | | | | | |
| University of Pisa | 1 | | 0.1 | 1 | 100 | | | 1 | | | | | | |
| | | | | | | | | | | | | | | |
| **Western Europe** | | | | | | | | | | | | | | |
| Austria | | | | | | | | | | | | | | |
| University of Vienna | 1 | | 0.1 | 1 | 100 | | | 1 | | | | | | |
| Technical University of Vienna | 1 | | 0.1 | | | 1 | 100 | 1 | | | | | | |
| | | | | | | | | | | | | | | |
| Belgium | | | | | | | | | | | | | | |
| Free University | 1 | | 0.1 | | | 1 | 100 | 1 | | | | | | |
| | | | | | | | | | | | | | | |
| France | | | | | | | | | | | | | | |
| ÉcoleNationaleSupérieure des Arts de la Marionnette | 1 | | 0.1 | 1 | 100 | | | 1 | | | | | | |
| ÉcoleNormaleSupérieure, Paris | 1 | | 0.1 | 1 | 100 | | | 1 | | | | | | |
| Université de Paris | 1 | | 0.1 | 1 | 100 | | | 1 | | | | | | |
| Ecole des Hautes Etudes en Sciences Sociales | 1 | | 0.1 | 1 | 100 | | | 1 | | | | | | |
| Université Pierre et Marie Curie | 1 | | 0.1 | 1 | 100 | | | 1 | | | | | | |
| Total | 5 | | 0.5 | 5 | 100 | | | 5 | | | | | | |
| | | | | | | | | | | | | | | |
| Germany | | | | | | | | | | | | | | |
| Ludwig-Maximilians-Universität | 1 | | 0.1 | 1 | 100 | | | 1 | | | | | | |
| University of Heidelberg | 1 | | 0.1 | 1 | 100 | | | 1 | | | | | | |
| University of Berlin | 1 | | 0.1 | 1 | 100 | | | 1 | | | | | | |
| University of Frankfurt | 1 | | 0.1 | 1 | 100 | | | 1 | | | | | | |
| University of Göttingen | 1 | | 0.1 | 1 | 100 | | | 1 | | | | | | |
| University of Hamburg | 2 | | 0.2 | 2 | 100 | | | 2 | | | | | | |
| University of Tübingen | 1 | | 0.1 | 1 | 100 | | | | | 1 | | | | |

| | | | | | | | | | | | | | |
|---|---|---|---|---|---|---|---|---|---|---|---|---|---|
| Total | 8 | | 0.83 | 8 | | | | 7 | | 1 | | | |
| | | | | | | | | | | | | | |
| Switzerland | | | | | | | | | | | | | |
| University of Bern | 1 | | 0.1 | 1 | 100 | | | 1 | | | | | |
| University of Geneva | 1 | | 0.1 | 1 | 100 | | | 1 | | | | | |
| | | | | | | | | | | | | | |
| Total | 18 | | 1.9 | 16 | 88.9 | 2 | 11.1 | 15 | 2 | 1 | | | |
| | | | | | | | | | | | | | |
| Europe Total | 78 | | 8.1 | 63 | 80.8 | 15 | 19.2 | 56 | 13 | 4 | 1 | 3 | 1 |
| % of all Fellows | | | | 6.5 | | 1.6 | | 5.8 | 1.3 | 0.4 | 0.1 | 0.3 | 0.1 |
| | | | | | | | | | | | | | |
| Latin America & Caribbean | | | | | | | | | | | | | |
| | | | | | | | | | | | | | |
| Caribbean | | | | | | | | | | | | | |
| Dominican Republic | | | | | | | | | | | | | |
| Universidad Catolica Madre y Maestra | 1 | | 0.1 | 1 | 100 | | | 1 | | | | | |
| | | | | | | | | | | | | | |
| Jamaica | | | | | | | | | | | | | |
| University of the West Indies | 1 | | 0.1 | 1 | 100 | | | | 1 | | | | |
| | | | | | | | | | | | | | |
| Total | 2 | | 0.2 | 2 | 100 | | | 1 | 1 | | | | |
| | | | | | | | | | | | | | |
| Central America | | | | | | | | | | | | | |
| | | | | | | | | | | | | | |
| Mexico | | | | | | | | | | | | | |
| Instituto Allende | 1 | | 0.1 | | | 1 | 100 | | | 1 | | | |
| | | | | | | | | | | | | | |
| South America | | | | | | | | | | | | | |
| | | | | | | | | | | | | | |
| Chile | | | | | | | | | | | | | |
| University of Chile in Santiago | 1 | | 0.1 | 1 | 100 | | | 1 | | | | | |
| | | | | | | | | | | | | | |
| Argentina | | | | | | | | | | | | | |
| University of Buenos Aires | 1 | | 0.1 | | 0 | 1 | 100 | | 1 | | | | |
| Total | 2 | | 0.2 | 1 | 50 | 1 | 50 | 1 | | | | | |
| | | | | | | | | | | | | | |
| Latin America & Caribbean Total | 5 | | 0.52 | 3 | 60 | 2 | 40 | 2 | 1 | 1 | 1 | | |

| | | | | | | | | | | | | | |
|---|---|---|---|---|---|---|---|---|---|---|---|---|---|
| % of all Fellows | | | 0.3 | | 0.2 | | 0.2 | | 0.1 | 0.1 | | | |
| | | | | | | | | | | | | | |
| Oceania | | | | | | | | | | | | | | 
| Australia | | | | | | | | | | | | | |
| Australian National University | 1 | | 0.1 | 1 | 100 | | | 1 | | | | | |
| University of elbourne | 1 | | 0.1 | 1 | 100 | | | 1 | | | | | |
| University of New England, New South Wales | 1 | | 0.1 | 1 | 100 | | | 1 | | | | | |
| Total | 3 | | 0.3 | 3 | 100 | | | 3 | | | | | |
| % of all Fellows | | | | 0.3 | | | | 0.3 | | | | | |
| | | | | | | | | | | | | | |
| All Fellows | 965 | | | 593 | 61.451 | 372 | 38.55 | 490 | 293 | 60 | 50 | 39 | 21 | 4 | 8 |
| % of all Fellows | | | | | | | | 50.8 | 30.4 | 6.2 | 5.2 | 4.0 | 2.2 | 0.4 | 0.8 |

Source: Compiled and computed based on data provided by the MacArthur Fellows Program (June 2017 to February 2019) at: https://www.macfound.org/fellows/search/all.

## Year of Graduation of Earned Highest/Terminal Higher Education Degrees of MacArthur Fellows, 1981 to 2018, by Sex and Race

The year of graduation for the highest or terminal degrees earned by MacArthur Fellows is information that can be useful to the understanding of the American society. It tells a story of the gradual degree attainment of women and minorities in the past century. Table 9 presents the year of graduation for highest or terminal degrees of MacArthur Fellows. Of the 965 degrees earned, the year of graduation is missing for one Asian man, with 964 remaining.

Table 9 shows that a degree was earned in 1923 and 3 degrees were earned in 2017. Of the 7 degrees earned in 5 different years in the 1920s, 6 were earned by White men and only 1 was earned by a White woman in 1927. Table 9 shows that it was in 1938 when the first non-White Fellow earned a degree (a Black woman). The highest number of degrees earned in a year is in 1971 and 1980, each with 30. For the 30 degrees earned in 1971 (21 degrees earned by men and 9 degrees earned by women), 18 are earned by White men, 8 by White women, 2 by Black men, and 1 each by a Black woman and an Asian man. Of the 30 degrees earned in 1980 (22 by men and 8 by women), 21 are earned by White men, 7 by White women, and 1 each by an Asian man and a Black woman. The highest number of degrees earned in a year by men is 22 in 1980; 13 degrees each by women in 1993 and 2003; 21 by White men in 1980; 10 each in 1982 and 2001 by White women; 5 by Black men in 1997; 4 by Black women in 1984; 5 by Asian men in 1998; 3 each in 1996 and 1998 by Asian women; 1 each by Native American men in 1967, 1983, 1999, and 2000; and 1 each by Native American women in 1951, 1964, 1969, 1984, 1994, 1995, 2000, and 2006 (Table 9).

**Table 9. Year of Graduation for Earned Highest/Terminal Higher Education Degrees of MacArthur Fellows, 1981 to 2018, by Sex and Race**
**Note:** WM = White men; WW = White women; BM = Black men; BW = Black women; AM = Asian men; AW = Asian women; NAM = Native American men; NAW = Native American women

| Year | # | % Total | Men | % Total | Women | % Total | WM | WW | BM | BW | AM | AW | NAM | NAW |
|---|---|---|---|---|---|---|---|---|---|---|---|---|---|---|
| 1923 | 1 | 0.104 | 1 | 0.1 | | | 1 | | | | | | | |
| 1926 | 1 | 0.104 | 1 | 0.1 | | | 1 | | | | | | | |
| 1927 | 3 | 0.311 | 2 | 0.2 | 1 | 0.104 | 2 | 1 | | | | | | |
| 1928 | 1 | 0.104 | 1 | 0.1 | | | 1 | | | | | | | |
| 1929 | 1 | 0.104 | 1 | 0.1 | | | 1 | | | | | | | |
| 1931 | 2 | 0.207 | 2 | 0.2 | | | 2 | | | | | | | |
| 1933 | 1 | 0.104 | 1 | 0.1 | | | 1 | | | | | | | |
| 1935 | 1 | 0.104 | 1 | 0.1 | | | 1 | | | | | | | |
| 1936 | 1 | 0.104 | 1 | 0.1 | | | 1 | | | | | | | |
| 1937 | 1 | 0.104 | 1 | 0.1 | | | 1 | | | | | | | |
| 1938 | 1 | 0.104 | | | 1 | 0.104 | | | | 1 | | | | |
| 1939 | 1 | 0.104 | | | 1 | 0.104 | | 1 | | | | | | |
| 1940 | 3 | 0.311 | 3 | 0.3 | | | 3 | | | | | | | |
| 1941 | 2 | 0.207 | | | 2 | 0.207 | | 2 | | | | | | |
| 1942 | 1 | 0.104 | 1 | 0.1 | | | 1 | | | | | | | |
| 1944 | 2 | 0.207 | 1 | 0.1 | 1 | 0.104 | 1 | | | 1 | | | | |
| 1946 | 1 | 0.104 | 1 | 0.1 | | | 1 | | | | | | | |
| 1948 | 2 | 0.207 | 1 | 0.1 | 1 | 0.104 | 1 | 1 | | | | | | |
| 1949 | 5 | 0.519 | 5 | 0.5 | | | 5 | | | | | | | |

| 1950 | 1 | 0.104 | 1 | 0.1 | | | 1 | | | | | | |
|---|---|---|---|---|---|---|---|---|---|---|---|---|---|
| 1951 | 10 | 1.037 | 6 | 0.6 | 4 | 0.415 | 4 | 3 | 1 | | 1 | | | 1 |
| 1952 | 2 | 0.207 | 2 | 0.2 | | | 2 | | | | | | |
| 1953 | 6 | 0.622 | 5 | 0.5 | 1 | 0.104 | 4 | | 1 | 1 | | | |
| 1954 | 5 | 0.519 | 4 | 0.4 | 1 | 0.104 | 3 | 1 | 1 | | | | |
| 1955 | 8 | 0.83 | 4 | 0.4 | 4 | 0.415 | 4 | 4 | | | | | |
| 1956 | 7 | 0.726 | 7 | 0.7 | | | 7 | | | | | | |
| 1957 | 6 | 0.622 | 5 | 0.5 | 1 | 0.104 | 3 | 1 | 2 | | | | |
| 1958 | 10 | 1.037 | 7 | 0.7 | 3 | 0.311 | 7 | 3 | | | | | |
| 1959 | 8 | 0.83 | 8 | 0.8 | | | 7 | | 1 | | | | |
| 1960 | 11 | 1.141 | 11 | 1.1 | | | 11 | | | | | | |
| 1961 | 7 | 0.726 | 7 | 0.7 | | | 6 | | | 1 | | | |
| 1962 | 13 | 1.349 | 11 | 1.1 | 2 | 0.207 | 8 | 2 | 2 | | 1 | | |
| 1963 | 15 | 1.556 | 12 | 1.2 | 3 | 0.311 | 10 | 2 | 1 | 1 | 1 | | |
| 1964 | 9 | 0.934 | 4 | 0.4 | 5 | 0.519 | 4 | 4 | | | | | 1 |
| 1965 | 17 | 1.763 | 13 | 1.3 | 4 | 0.415 | 11 | 4 | 2 | | | | |
| 1966 | 20 | 2.075 | 12 | 1.2 | 8 | 0.83 | 9 | 8 | 3 | | | | |
| 1967 | 24 | 2.49 | 21 | 2.2 | 3 | 0.311 | 19 | 3 | 1 | | | 1 | |
| 1968 | 14 | 1.452 | 9 | 0.9 | 5 | 0.519 | 8 | 4 | 1 | 1 | | | |
| 1969 | 17 | 1.763 | 12 | 1.2 | 5 | 0.519 | 11 | 3 | 1 | 1 | | | 1 |
| 1970 | 17 | 1.763 | 10 | 1.0 | 7 | 0.726 | 10 | 7 | | | | | |
| 1971 | 30 | 3.112 | 21 | 2.2 | 9 | 0.934 | 18 | 8 | 2 | 1 | 1 | | |
| 1972 | 19 | 1.971 | 8 | 0.8 | 11 | 1.141 | 8 | 8 | | 3 | | | |
| 1973 | 20 | 2.075 | 18 | 1.9 | 2 | 0.207 | 14 | 2 | 4 | | | | |
| 1974 | 20 | 2.075 | 12 | 1.2 | 8 | 0.83 | 11 | 8 | | | 1 | | |
| 1975 | 24 | 2.49 | 13 | 1.3 | 11 | 1.141 | 13 | 8 | | 3 | | | |
| 1976 | 25 | 2.593 | 17 | 1.8 | 8 | 0.83 | 13 | 8 | 4 | | | | |
| 1977 | 15 | 1.556 | 10 | 1.0 | 5 | 0.519 | 9 | 4 | | 1 | 1 | | |
| 1978 | 21 | 2.178 | 13 | 1.3 | 8 | 0.83 | 12 | 6 | 1 | 2 | | | |
| 1979 | 24 | 2.49 | 16 | 1.7 | 8 | 0.83 | 14 | 8 | 2 | | | | |
| 1980 | 30 | 3.112 | 22 | 2.3 | 8 | 0.83 | 21 | 7 | | 1 | 1 | | |
| 1981 | 13 | 1.349 | 9 | 0.9 | 4 | 0.415 | 7 | 4 | 2 | | | | |
| 1982 | 17 | 1.763 | 7 | 0.7 | 10 | 1.037 | 6 | 10 | 1 | | | | |

| Year | | | | | | | | | | | | | | |
|---|---|---|---|---|---|---|---|---|---|---|---|---|---|---|
| 1983 | 23 | 2.386 | 12 | 1.2 | 11 | 1.141 | 11 | 8 | | 2 | | 1 | 1 | |
| 1984 | 24 | 2.49 | 13 | 1.3 | 11 | 1.141 | 11 | 6 | 2 | 4 | | | | 1 |
| 1985 | 19 | 1.971 | 9 | 0.9 | 10 | 1.037 | 6 | 7 | 2 | 2 | 1 | 1 | | |
| 1986 | 10 | 1.037 | 3 | 0.3 | 7 | 0.726 | 3 | 7 | | | | | | |
| 1987 | 17 | 1.763 | 11 | 1.1 | 6 | 0.622 | 9 | 6 | | | 2 | | | |
| 1988 | 18 | 1.867 | 10 | 1.0 | 8 | 0.83 | 8 | 7 | 1 | 1 | 1 | | | |
| 1989 | 20 | 2.075 | 11 | 1.1 | 9 | 0.934 | 10 | 8 | | 1 | 1 | | | |
| 1990 | 18 | 1.867 | 11 | 1.1 | 7 | 0.726 | 11 | 7 | | | | | | |
| 1991 | 13 | 1.349 | 10 | 1.0 | 3 | 0.311 | 6 | 3 | 2 | | 2 | | | |
| 1992 | 16 | 1.66 | 8 | 0.8 | 8 | 0.83 | 8 | 8 | | | | | | |
| 1993 | 19 | 1.971 | 6 | 0.6 | 13 | 1.349 | 2 | 9 | 2 | 3 | 2 | 1 | | |
| 1994 | 18 | 1.867 | 6 | 0.6 | 12 | 1.245 | 6 | 9 | | 1 | | 1 | | 1 |
| 1995 | 21 | 2.178 | 12 | 1.2 | 9 | 0.934 | 9 | 5 | 1 | 1 | 2 | 2 | | 1 |
| 1996 | 14 | 1.452 | 6 | 0.6 | 8 | 0.83 | 5 | 3 | | 2 | 1 | 3 | | |
| 1997 | 24 | 2.49 | 14 | 1.5 | 10 | 1.037 | 7 | 7 | 5 | 2 | 2 | 1 | | |
| 1998 | 22 | 2.282 | 13 | 1.3 | 9 | 0.934 | 7 | 6 | 1 | | 5 | 3 | | |
| 1999 | 19 | 1.971 | 11 | 1.1 | 8 | 0.83 | 6 | 6 | 1 | 1 | 3 | 1 | 1 | |
| 2000 | 13 | 1.349 | 6 | 0.6 | 7 | 0.726 | 4 | 2 | 1 | 3 | | 1 | 1 | 1 |
| 2001 | 21 | 2.178 | 9 | 0.9 | 12 | 1.245 | 9 | 10 | | 2 | | | | |
| 2002 | 10 | 1.037 | 7 | 0.7 | 3 | 0.311 | 5 | 1 | 1 | | 1 | 2 | | |
| 2003 | 21 | 2.178 | 8 | 0.8 | 13 | 1.349 | 4 | 9 | 1 | 2 | 3 | 2 | | |
| 2004 | 9 | 0.934 | 3 | 0.3 | 6 | 0.622 | 3 | 6 | | | | | | |
| 2005 | 12 | 1.245 | 7 | 0.7 | 5 | 0.519 | 4 | 3 | 2 | 1 | 1 | 1 | | |
| 2006 | 9 | 0.934 | 5 | 0.5 | 4 | 0.415 | 3 | 2 | 2 | | | 1 | | 1 |
| 2007 | 7 | 0.726 | 5 | 0.5 | 2 | 0.207 | 2 | 1 | 2 | 1 | 1 | | | |
| 2008 | 6 | 0.622 | 4 | 0.4 | 2 | 0.207 | 2 | 1 | | 1 | 2 | | | |
| 2009 | 9 | 0.934 | 5 | 0.5 | 4 | 0.415 | 5 | 4 | | | | | | |
| 2010 | 5 | 0.519 | 2 | 0.2 | 3 | 0.311 | 2 | 3 | | | | | | |
| 2011 | 5 | 0.519 | 1 | 0.1 | 4 | 0.415 | 1 | 2 | | 2 | | | | |
| 2012 | 3 | 0.311 | 1 | 0.1 | 2 | 0.207 | 1 | 2 | | | | | | |
| 2017 | 3 | 0.311 | 2 | 0.2 | 1 | 0.104 | 1 | | | 1 | 1 | | | |
| Total | 964 | 100 | 592 | 61.4 | 372 | 38.59 | 490 | 293 | 60 | 50 | 38 | 21 | 4 | 8 |
| % of all Fellows | | | | | | | 50.8 | 30.4 | 6.2 | 5.19 | 3.94 | 2.2 | 0.415 | 0.83 |

Source: Compiled and computed based on data provided by the MacArthur Fellows Program (June 2017 to February 2019) at: https://www.macfound.org/fellows/search/all.

# CHAPTER FIVE

## Discussion

The statistics on the MacArthur Fellows presented above, which might seem disparate, have provided to the public with a better understanding of the demographic, educational, and professional backgrounds of these geniuses and creativists. The data illustrated that while White men accounted for the majority of Fellows selected from 1981 to 2018, women and minorities have substantially increased their overall proportions. Since the data show that those selected to be Fellows are aged 18 and older, the 12.5% of Blacks and the 5.9% of Asians in Table 1 are almost their adult proportions in the general population of the United States discussed above Table 5. For example, of the 249.2 million people in the United States aged 18 and over in 2018, 13.3% were Black and 6.2% were Asian. The 1.995 million Native Americans aged 18 and over in 2017 discussed above Table 5 is 0.8% of the 247.4 million people aged 18 and over in the United States in that year.

However, as the data illustrated, the figures have not increased for women, especially Asian, Black, and White women, the way they have increased for minorities. For example, as Table 1 shows, women accounted for 37.2% of all Fellows selected from 1981 to 2018: 29.1% of White Women, 5.3% of Black women, 1.98% of Asian women, and 0.8% of Native American women. However, as noted above Table 5, in 2018, women accounted for 51.6% of people aged 18 and over in the United States: 32.5% non-Hispanic White women, 7.2% Black women, and 3.3% Asian women. These findings are consistent with other studies of prominent people in the United States, including some in this current study, whereby for the most part, regardless of race, women are a visible minority (Coutu, 2007; "'Honey, You Got a MacArthur': Blacks Who Have Received the Coveted Genius Grant," 1997; Kaba, 2012b, 2013ab, 2015, 2016, 2017; Miller et al., 2018; Pick, 1995; Wooster 2010, p.43).

The study by Kaba (2012b) of the 2011 *Root Magazine's* 100 most influential young Black Americans aged 25 to 45 showed that 66 of them were men and 34 were women. The *Root Magazine* is a prominent Black American magazine. These individuals are among the most prominent

Black Americans, including several current members of the U.S. Congress (including the U.S. Senate), cabinet members of the federal government, mayors of large cities, professional athletes, religious leaders, entertainers, entrepreneurs, etc. (pp.5-7). Kaba's (2013b) study of the contributors of full-length articles to the *American Sociological Review*, the top sociology journal in the United States, showed that of the 80 total contributors to all issues of the journal in 2010, men accounted for 61 (63.7%) and women accounted for 29 (36.3%). This same study presents data for 2010 for the contributors to the *American Economic Review*, the top economics journal in the United States, and showed that male contributors of full-length articles accounted for 194 (87.4%) of the 222 contributors and women accounted for 28 (12.6%). For the *American Political Science Review*, the top political science journal in the United States, male contributors accounted for 68 (86.1%) of all 79 contributors to the journal in 2010, and women accounted for 11 (13.9%) (pp. 122-125). In Kaba's (2017a) study of America's great immigrants, of the 408 honorees from 2006 to 2015, men accounted for 289 (70.8%) and women accounted for 119 (29.2%). These are among the most prominent or successful people in the United States. Data for 122 of them showed that their total net worth in 2017 was $113.4 billion. Of the 122 honorees, men accounted for 87 (71.3%), with a total net worth of $106.9 (94.3%) billion, and women accounted for 35 (28.7%), with a total net worth of $6.51 (5.7%) billion (pp.24 & 101). In an interview with a former Director of the MacArthur Fellows Program, Daniel J. Socolow, Coutu (2007) brought up this issue:

> Do women have greater difficulty winning a MacArthur?
> The number of woman fellows has increased significantly over time as women's roles in society have shifted. Women are still not nominated as frequently as men, even though we work hard to ensure that they are as well represented among the nominators. Women are every bit as creative as men—just look at those who do receive MacArthur fellowships each year. It is possible that differences in career paths and competing demands on their time still hold women back from taking unconventional directions and challenging accepted boundaries. The gap in numbers of nominations is closing, however, and that is encouraging. Personally, I get very excited when a majority of women are selected as fellows in a particular year. That's happened only once in my ten years here and only a couple of times before that. But the numbers of men and women are usually very close now (p.126).

Females tend to have more associate, bachelor's, and master's degrees than their male counterparts, but they have fewer professional and doctoral degrees than their male counterparts. The reason for this is that foreign-born males tend to earn a substantial proportion of professional and doctoral degrees. For example, in 2019, of the 10.381 million people with associate degrees (occupational) in the United States aged 18 and over, females accounted for 5.572 (53.7%) million; 8.220 (58%) million of the 14.168 million associate degrees (academic); 28.106 (52.7%) million of the 53.312 million bachelor's degrees; 12.738 (56.7%) million of the 22.459 million master's degrees; 1.324 (42%) million of the 3.150 million professional degrees; and 1.960 (43%) million of the 4.557 million doctoral degrees ("Table 1. Educational Attainment of the Population 18 Years and Over," 2020). However, for Black alone or in a combination of another race in the United States, females had more degrees in all levels: 762,000 (57%) out of 1.338 associate degrees (occupational); 1.162 (60.3%) million of the 1.926 million associate degrees (academic); 2.910 (55.7%) million out of 5.229 million bachelor's degrees; 1.510 (66.3%) million out of 2.279 million master's degrees; 134,000 (67.3%) out of 199,000 professional degrees; and 173,000 (56.9%) out of 304,000 doctoral degrees ("Table 1. Educational Attainment of the Population 18 Years and Over," 2020).

However, among individuals who earn doctoral degrees, males with temporary visa status in the United States have a substantial proportion of the total. For example, each year from 2009 to 2018, male temporary visa holders earned more doctoral degrees than their female counterparts, and they also accounted for a substantial proportion of all doctoral degrees awarded. In 2018, of the 29,798 doctoral degrees awarded to males by colleges and universities in the United States, U.S. citizens and permanent residents accounted for 17,335 (58.2%) and temporary visa holders accounted for 11,322 (38%) ("Table 20. Male doctorate recipients, by ethnicity, race, and citizenship status: 2009–18," 2020). In 2018, of the 25,368 doctoral degrees awarded to females by colleges and universities in the United States, U.S. citizens and permanent residents accounted for 18,068 (71.2%) and temporary visa holders accounted for 6,282 (24.8%) ("Table 21. Female doctorate recipients, by ethnicity, race, and citizenship status: 2009–18," 2020).

For Black Americans, while more female citizens and permanent residents have more doctoral degrees than their male counterparts each year from 2009 to 2018, more male temporary visa holders had more doctoral degrees than their female counterparts. For example, In 2018, of the 1,730 doctoral degrees awarded to Black females by colleges and universities in the United States, U.S. citizens and permanent residents accounted for 1,530 (88.4%) and temporary visa holders accounted for 197 (11.4%) ("Table 21. Female doctorate recipients, by ethnicity, race, and citizenship status: 2009–18," 2020). In 2018, of the 1,328 doctoral degrees awarded to Black males by colleges and universities in the United States, U.S. citizens and permanent residents accounted for 926 (69.7%) and temporary visa holders accounted for 399 (30.1%) ("Table 20. Male doctorate recipients, by ethnicity, race, and citizenship status: 2009–18," 2020).

For the remaining part of this discussion section, the following findings from this study are examined: the complex racial categorization in the United States; Asian Fellows as the youngest racial group; first name; educational attainment and highest or terminal degrees; educational attainment and academic institutions; academic institutions and geographic location; and the location at the time of award versus place of birth.

**Complex Racial Categorization in the United States**

It is important to point out that the method used to define racial categories in the United States is responsible for Whites accounting for over four out of every five Fellows in this current study. As noted in the methodology section, most individuals from Arab countries in Asia and Africa are categorized as White in the United States; individuals from Iran, Israel, Turkey, and most central Asian nations are also categorized as White. Individuals from China, Japan, South Korea, India, and Southeastern Asian nations are categorized as Asian, but if any of them has a child with someone who is categorized as White, such as an Irish person, then that child is White. One such person is categorized as White in this study, instead of Asian. As the place of birth data in Table 2 shows, four of the five Fellows born in Northern Africa are White, even though they are Arab, and all 10 Fellows born in Western Asia are White. It is highly likely that a significant to substantial proportion of the 151 Fellows born in New York state, in particular, could have direct ancestry from Western Asian nations such as Israel, Jordan, Lebanon, Syria, or Turkey; or they could have ancestry from North African nations such as Egypt, Libya, Morocco, or Tunisia. This means that the method of racial categorization in the United States tends to hide the Asian population in the United States, which then results in those Asian and African nations not getting the recognition they deserve -- because most people equate White with European. Kaba (2017a) discussed this issue and pointed out that the Barack Obama administration published a notice in the Federal Register entitled:

> Standards for Maintaining, Collecting and Presenting Federal Data on Race and Ethnicity" for the public to make comments on the government's intention to create a new racial category in the 2020 U.S. Census called: "Middle Eastern and North African" (MENA). It is reported that this potential racial categorization "… would include anyone from a region of the world stretching from Morocco to Iran, and including Syrian and Coptic Christians, Israeli Jews and other religious minorities (pp.105-106).

This study helps to solve this important problem by presenting the place of birth data of the Fellows. Although a person from any racial or ethnic ancestry may be born anywhere, the country of birth data for the 220 Fellows born outside of the United States showed that most of them were actually born in their ancestry lands, outside of Europe. This then gives recognition to those societies for the important contributions that their daughters and sons have made, and that they are not just counted as White, which is equated to European in the United States.

**Asian Fellows as the Youngest Racial Group**

While the oldest and youngest Fellows selected are White men, and the youngest woman selected is a Black woman, Asians on average are the youngest group. Two interrelated reasons could be cited for this fact: immigration and their relatively small population in the country, despite a substantial percentage increase in their immigration to the United States in the past 15 years. As illustrated in a paragraph above, there are more Black women aged 18 and over (7.2%) and just as many Black men (5.9%) aged 18 and over than the total Asian population aged 18 and over in the United States (6.2%). Asians started arriving in the United

States in significant numbers after the 1965 Immigration Act, which opened up the country to immigrants from most parts of the world (Kaba, 2019; Young, 2017: 226). As Table 2 shows, of the 60 Asian Fellows in this current study, 17 (28.3%) were born in the United States: 16 (26.7%) were born in China; 10 (16.7%) were born in India; 4 (6.7%) each were born in Japan and Vietnam, and 3 (5%) were born in Pakistan. In addition, the Fellowship is also awarded to citizens and permanent residents of the United States. As Conrad (2014, September 3) points out, data on MacArthur Fellows "… highlight the contribution of immigrants to the creative culture of the United States. Nearly a quarter of MacArthur Fellows were born outside of the country. Though Fellows must be citizens or residents of the United States, their countries of origin span the globe."

The relative youth of Asian Fellows compared with Fellows from other racial or ethnic groups is also connected to educational attainment and immigration. Asian Fellows have the highest rate of terminal degrees in this study, a fact connected to their immigration status. For example, in 2018, of the 8,908 doctoral degrees awarded to Asian males by colleges and universities in the United States, U.S. citizens and permanent residents accounted for 1,563 (17.6%) and temporary visa holders accounted for 7,320 (82.2%). The 7,320 doctoral degrees earned by male Asian temporary visa holders in 2018 accounted for 24.6% of the 29,798 doctoral degrees awarded to all males ("Table 20. Male doctorate recipients, by ethnicity, race, and citizenship status: 2009–18," 2020). In 2018, of the 5,907 doctoral degrees awarded to Asian females by colleges and universities in the United States, U.S. citizens and permanent residents accounted for 1,742 (29.5%) and temporary visa holders accounted for 4,155 (70.3%). The 4,155 doctoral degrees earned by female Asian temporary visa holders in 2018 accounted for 16.4% of the 25,368 doctoral degrees awarded to all females ("Table 21. Female doctorate recipients, by ethnicity, race, and citizenship status: 2009–18," 2020).

An ancestral breakdown of Asians reveals that, of the 60 Fellows, 18 (30%) are Indian men; 16 (26.7%) are Chinese men; 12 (20%) are Chinese women; 3 (5%) each are Japanese and Pakistani women; 2 (3.3%) each are Japanese and Vietnamese men; and 1 (1.7%) each is a Cambodian man, a South Korean man, and a Vietnamese woman (Compiled from Table 2). It is important to note that while it is surprising that no Indian woman with ancestry from India has been selected by 2018, in 2019, of the 26 individuals selected as Fellows, one is an Indian woman ("2019 MacArthur Fellows," 2019).

**First Names**

To some extent, one could make a connection to the first names findings in this study to the ancestral backgrounds of the Fellows. The first name data show that among men, the most common names are John, 35(5.5%), David, 33 (5.2%), Robert, 22 (3.5%), Michael, 19 (3%), Peter, 17 (2.7%),William, 15 (2.4%), James, 11 (1.7%), and Paul, 10 (1.5%). For women, the most common first names are Susan, 11 (2.9%), Nancy, 7 (1.9%), and Deborah, Julie, Patricia, and Rebecca, 6 (1.6%) each (Tables 3ab).*The New York Times* study cited in the methodology section on the first names of prominent political, legal, entertainment, and corporate leaders in the United States highlights the importance of this phenomenon: "In the corridors of American power, it can be as easy to find a man named John as it is to find a woman…." Examples from several important sectors of the American society support this claim: "Fewer Republican senators are women than men named John — despite the fact that Johns represent 3.3% of the male population, while women represent 50.8 percent of the total population. Fewer Democratic governors are women than men named John. And fewer women directed the top-grossing 100 films last year than men named Michael and James combined"(Miller et al., 2018; also see **Wuffle and Coulter, 2014:174**). Indeed, in this current study, the 35 Fellows named John account for 9.3% of the 377 women in the study (Tables 3a and b).

Carneiro et al. (2020) point to studies that: "used a variety of empirical strategies to show that the adoption of American sounding first names led to substantial improvements in labor market outcomes of first and second generation immigrants. Their conjecture is that this is due to a more successful assimilation process by those with American names. In spite of the benefits to adopting an American name, 20 to 30% of all immigrants in the 1900-1930 Censuses decided to keep a foreign name" (p.1).

Carneiro et al. (2020) find in their study that, in the 1900, 1910, 1920, and 1930 United States censuses, the top 10 popular male names by country of birth for 16 countries, had John in the top 10 from the following 14 countries: Germany (9.9%, ranked first), former USSR

(4.8%, ranked first), Poland (12.2%, ranked first), Sweden (13.8%, ranked first), Norway (9.3%, ranked first), Hungary (16.7%, ranked first), Czechoslovakia (18.6%, ranked first), and France (7.2%, ranked first); Greece (10.6%, ranked second) and Portugal (12.4%, ranked second); Italy (6.4%, ranked third) and Denmark (6%, ranked third); Spain (4.4%, ranked fourth); Mexico (1.6%, ranked ninth); and Japan (0.3% ranked sixth). China is the only country of the 16 listed where John was not in the top 10.

For female names during this same years and countries, the name Mary was in the top 10 in 15 of the 16 countries listed, excluding Japan: Germany (9.4%, ranked first), Italy (15.3%, ranked first), former USSR (5.8%, ranked first), Poland (15.1%, ranked first), Sweden (4.1%, ranked third), Norway (5.2%, ranked second), Hungary (16.7%, ranked first), Czechoslovakia (24.9%, ranked first), and France (10.1%, ranked first); Greece (12.6%, ranked first) and Portugal (37.4%, ranked first); and Denmark (9.4%, ranked second); Spain (10.1%, ranked first); and China (0.9% ranked tenth), Mexico (3.2%, ranked fourth) (pp.4-5).

The information presented in this section shows that the first name of an individual in the United States, in particular, may determine that person's overall success in society. The fact that individuals with certain first names just happen to hold influential positions in society means that it is not a coincidence. This has implications in society because it will influence how parents name their children, even if they are put in a position to go against their religious or cultural naming rituals.

## Educational Attainment and Highest or Terminal Degrees

Educational attainment, especially terminal degrees such as doctoral, MDs, JDs, and to a great extent, master's degrees, tend to be the primary factor for the selection of an individual as a MacArthur Fellow. This is especially the case with the PhD. degree, which turns out to account for 514 (53.3%) of the total 965 terminal or highest degrees awarded to 928 Fellows.The 144 bachelor's degrees earned by 140 Fellows, plus the 3 associate/diploma degrees earned by 3 Fellows, which combined for 147 degrees, account for 15.2% of all 965 degrees awarded. It is important to note that while earning a college degree, especially terminal degrees, is a big factor that determines an individual's selection to become a MacArthur Fellow. As discussed above Table 8 by the Fellows Program itself, a substantial proportion of Fellows did not earn a college degree or did not attend college altogether. This brings us to the terms genius and creativity discussed in the conceptual definition section of this study. While the media and the general public identify the Fellows as geniuses, the MacArthur Fellows program uses the term creative to describe them. In fact, the title of the 2019 announcement of the new Fellows has the word creative in it: "Meet the 2019 MacArthur Fellows: 26 Extraordinarily Creative People Who Inspire Us All."(https://www.macfound.org/videos/650/). This means that both the public and the MacArthur Fellows program appreciate talented or highly skilled individuals, regardless of whether they earned a college degree or not.

Although earning a terminal degree increases a person's chances of being selected as a MacArthur Fellow, in the United States, in particular, the higher education institutions where Fellows earned their degrees can be argued to be far more important than the degree itself. Table 10 substantiates this argument. For example, the eight Ivy League institutions combined (Brown University, Columbia University, Cornell University, Dartmouth College, Harvard University, Princeton University, the University of Pennsylvania, and Yale University) in the United States awarded 306 (31.7%) of the total 965 degrees to 300 Fellows (32.3%) (190 degrees earned by 185 men, and 116 degrees earned by 115 women): 2 White men had 2 degrees each from Harvard University; 1 White man had 2 degrees from the University of Pennsylvania; 1 White man had 1 degree each from Princeton University and Yale University; and 1 Asian man and 1 White woman each had 2 degrees from Harvard University (Table 10; also see Benzon, 2018: 4&7; Wooster, 2010:42).

Writing about the predominance of Princeton University among MacArthur Fellows despite having a total student enrollment of only 8,213 (undergraduate and graduate) as of November 30, 2019, on its website, Wooster (2010) notes that: "For some reason, an inordinate number of fellowships had been awarded to scholars at Princeton University, including seven in the first two years. By 1987, five MacArthur Fellows—physicist Joseph H. Taylor, historian Robert Darnton, physicist Edward Witten, astrophysicist James Gunn, and physicist David Gross—were all Princeton professors who lived on Hartley Avenue" (p.42). Kaba's (2012b) study of the top 100 most influential young Black Americans aged 25 to 45 showed that 70 of them earned 72 bachelor's degrees; 31 of them earned 35 master's degrees; 13

of them earned 13 Juris Doctorate degrees; and 9 of them earned 10 doctoral degrees, including an MD. The study points out that seven of the eight Ivy League institutions in the United States (Brown University, Dartmouth College, Columbia University, Harvard University, Princeton University, University of Pennsylvania, and Yale University) (excluding only Cornell University) awarded dozens of higher education degrees (bachelor's, master's, JD, and doctoral degrees) to those young influential Black Americans (pp. 18-25; also see Kaba, 2016:23-25). In addition, a study by Kaba (2009) of the *Journal of Blacks in Higher Education* most cited Black scholars in the social sciences, arts, and humanities in 2009, finds that of the 58 scholars and professors, 56 were employed at colleges and universities in the United States, with one employed in the United Kingdom. Of the 56 scholars and professors, 26 (46.5%) were employed at Ivy League institutions (18 men and 8 women) (pp. 163 & 165). Also, of the 58 scholars and professors in the study, 17 (29.2%) earned their terminal or highest degrees from Ivy League institutions (9 men and 8 women) (Kaba, 2009: 172). A study of 129 Black endowed professors in higher education institutions in the United States showed that 7 were employed at Harvard University, and 5 each were employed at Princeton University and the University of Pennsylvania (Stone, 2001: 121). Of the 51 contributors of full-length articles to all 2010 issues of the *American Sociological Review*, 19 (37.3%) were based at Ivy League institutions (Kaba, 2015:134).

Table 10. Number of Highest or Terminal Degrees Awarded by Ivy League Institutions to MacArthur Fellows, 1981-2018
n= 306 degrees awarded to 300 Fellows.

| Institution | Number of Degrees | Men | % of Ivy League Total | Women | % of Ivy League Total |
|---|---|---|---|---|---|
| Brown University | 7 | 3 | 0.98 | 4 | 1.3 |
| Columbia University | 44 | 26 | 8.5 | 18 | 5.9 |
| Cornell University | 20 | 12 | 3.9 | 8 | 2.6 |
| Dartmouth College | 2 | 1 | 0.33 | 1 | 0.33 |
| Harvard University | 119 | 79 | 25.8 | 40 | 13.1 |
| Princeton University | 41 | 27 | 8.8 | 14 | 4.6 |
| University of Pennsylvania | 12 | 8 | 2.6 | 4 | 1.3 |
| Yale University | 61 | 34 | 11.1 | 27 | 8.8 |
| Total | 306 | 190 | 62.1 | 116 | 37.9 |

Source: (Compiled and computed from Table 8 above).

A substantial number of institutions ranked in the *U.S. News and World Report* Top 50 to 75 national universities tend to have awarded 10 or more highest or terminal degrees to the Fellows in this current study. For example, the following top 25 institutions ranked in the 2020 *U.S. News and World Report* national rankings awarded 522 (54.1% of 965 degrees) degrees to 514 (55.4% of the 928 Fellows with highest or terminal degrees in this study) Fellows in this study: (#1) Princeton University (41 Fellows earned 42 degrees); (#2) Harvard University (115 Fellows earned 119 degrees, with 4 Fellows earning two degrees each, including 2 White men, 1 Asian man, and 1 White woman); (#3) Columbia University (44 Fellows earned 44 degrees), Massachusetts Institute of Technology (32 Fellows earning 32 degrees), and Yale University (61 Fellows earning 61 degrees) tie; (#6) Stanford University (20 Fellows earned 20 degrees), the University of Chicago (23 Fellows earned 24 degrees, including 1 White male who earned two degrees), and the University of Pennsylvania (11 Fellows earned 12 degrees, including 1 male who earned 2 degrees) tie; (#9) Northwestern University (5 Fellows earned 5 degrees); (#10) Duke University (6 Fellows earned 6 degrees) and Johns Hopkins University (15 Fellows earned 16 degrees, including 1 White male who earned 2 degrees) tie; (#12) California Institute of Technology (20 Fellows earned 20 degrees) and Dartmouth College (2 Fellows earned 2 degrees) tie; (#14) Brown University (7 Fellows earned 7 degrees); (#15) University of Notre Dame (no Fellow from this institution) and Vanderbilt University (2 Fellows earned 2 degrees) tie; (#17) Cornell University (20 Fellows earned 20 degrees) and Rice University (no Fellow from this institution) tie; (#19) Washington University in St. Louis (no Fellow from this institution); (#20) University of California, Los Angeles (17 Fellows earned 17 degrees); (#21) Emory University (1 Fellow earned a degree); (#22) University of California, Berkeley (51 Fellows earned 51 degrees) and the University of Southern California (4 Fellows earned 4 degrees) tie; (#24) Georgetown University (1 Fellow earned a degree); and (#25) Carnegie Mellon University (2 Fellows earned 2 degrees) and the University of Michigan, Ann Arbor(14 Fellows earned 14 degrees) tie (Table 11; also see Benzon, 2018: 4&7).

Table 11. Top 25 U.S. News and World Report National Universities and their Graduates Selected as MacArthur Fellows, 1981-2018

| 2020 U.S. News Rank | Institution | # of Fellows | # of Degrees |
|---|---|---|---|
| 1 | Princeton University | 41 | 42 |
| 2 | Harvard University | 115 | 119 |
| 3 | Columbia University | 44 | 44 |
| 3 | Massachusetts Institute of Technology | 32 | 32 |
| 3 | Yale University | 61 | 61 |
| 6 | Stanford University | 20 | 20 |
| 6 | University of Chicago | 23 | 24 |
| 6 | University of Pennsylvania | 11 | 12 |
| 9 | Northwestern University | 5 | 5 |
| 10 | Duke University | 6 | 6 |
| 10 | Johns Hopkins University | 15 | 16 |
| 12 | California Institute of Technology | 20 | 20 |
| 12 | Dartmouth College | 2 | 2 |
| 14 | Brown University | 7 | 7 |
| 15 | University of Notre Dame | 0 | 0 |
| 15 | Vanderbilt University | 2 | 2 |
| 17 | Cornell University | 20 | 20 |
| 17 | Rice University | 0 | 0 |
| 19 | Washington University in St. Louis | 0 | 0 |
| 20 | University of California, Los Angeles | 17 | 17 |
| 21 | Emory University | 1 | 1 |
| 22 | University of California, Berkeley | 51 | 51 |
| 22 | University of Southern California | 4 | 4 |
| 24 | Georgetown University | 1 | 1 |
| 25 | Carnegie Mellon University | 2 | 2 |
| 25 | University of Michigan, Ann Arbor | 14 | 14 |
| Total | | 514 | 522 |

Source: Compiled and computed from Table 8 above; and "National University Rankings, 2020," 2019.

## Geographic Location of Higher Education Institutions where MacArthur Fellows Earned their Highest or Terminal Degrees

This brings us to the geographic location such as the U.S. state and region, country, and world region where an institution is located. This is a piece of very important information that helps one to understand the selection of an individual as a Fellow. States and the four regions within the United States compete constantly for talented or gifted individuals. It is not a coincidence that all eight Ivy League institutions are located in the Northeast region of the United States, or that a substantial number of degrees (155 degrees) were awarded in California alone. The Northeast and the West, especially California tend to have relatively high numbers of Fellows partly because of their wealth, with New York, Massachusetts, and New Jersey leading the way in the Northeast. The wealthier a state and its region are, the more likely that they have significant numbers of top-ranked colleges and universities. This is because top-ranked institutions tend to have relatively high endowments. For example, Kaba's (2016) study finds that: ".... the endowment data provided by the US Department of Education for the 120 institutions in the US with the highest endowments in 2007 was $322.2 billion. The total for the eight Ivy League institutions in 2007 was $98.7 billion (30.6% of the $322.2 billion): Harvard University ($34.6 billion); Yale University ($22.5 billion); Princeton University ($15.8 billion); Columbia University $7.15 billion; University of Pennsylvania $6.64 billion; Cornell University $5.425 billion; Dartmouth College $ 3.76 billion; and Brown University $2.78 billion" (p.24). In California, in 2007, Stanford University alone had an endowment of $17.16 billion, and the California Institute of Technology, $1.86 billion (Kaba, 2012, p.28). This massive financial wealth owned by a university is also connected to the age of an institution. Kaba 's (2012) study also finds that the older an institution is, the more likely that it is highly ranked, and the more likely that it has a large endowment. For example, Ivy League institutions are among the oldest higher education institutions in the country, with Harvard University established in 1636, Yale University in 1701, and Princeton University in 1746 (p. 27).

These explanations in the paragraph above tend to apply for the most part to the countries with institutions that awarded the highest or terminal degrees to the Fellows in this current study. As Table 8 illustrates, The United Kingdom (8 institutions awarding 45 degrees), Germany (7 institutions awarding 8 degrees), and France (5 institutions awarding 5 degrees) have a significant number of institutions that awarded dozens of degrees to MacArthur Fellows. For example, the University of Oxford (established in 1096) awarded 18 degrees, the University of Cambridge (established in 1209), awarded 15 degrees, and the University of London (established in 1836), awarded 5 degrees. The University of Oxford is reported to have an endowment of 3.4 billion British pounds in 2007, and the University of Cambridge is reported to have an endowment of 4.1 billion British pounds in 2006 (Kaba, 2012a: p.27). Kaba (2012a) writes of these elite institutions: "Most of them have not just world-class medical degree programs, but also world-class hospitals attached to them. The political, economic, religious, and military elites in most countries of the world are trained at these institutions" (p.5).

The study by Han et al. (2015) examined the active recruitment of talented individuals back to their home countries (pp.4-5). Wadhwa (2009) writes of an Indian entrepreneur who recruited 100 highly skilled Indian nationals back to India, and that prominent United States corporations are recruiting highly skilled workers to their overseas locations (pp. 49-50). Teich (2014) points out that the United States is in active competition to recruit the best scientists and engineers in the world: "Countries that were minor players in science and technology a few years ago are rapidly entering the major leagues and actively pursuing scientific and technical talent in the global marketplace. The advent of rapid and inexpensive global communication and air travel that is within easy reach of researchers in many countries have fostered the growth of global networks of collaboration and are changing the way research is done (p.56). Shachar and Hirschl (2013) claim that developed or wealthy nations are intensely recruiting talented individuals (such as scientists and professional athletes) from all over the world. Some of the nations involved in this world-wide recruiting include Australia, Canada, China, Germany, New Zealand, Singapore, Taiwan, South Korea, the United Kingdom, and the United States. China is reported to be actively recruiting skilled individuals "As part of its One-Thousand-Talent program, China is also aggressively using financial, taxation, and membership perks to attract high-caliber international scholars and returning Chinese citizens to lead key laboratories, projects and disciplines in China" (p.84). Campanella (2015) discusses the challenges faced by European Union nations with the loss of their skilled workers recruited to work in Canada and the United States. For over five decades, these "... bright academics, ambitious entrepreneurs, and visionary scientists have defeated the conservatism of Europe by crossing the Atlantic Ocean in search of vibrant university environments and rewarding professional opportunities. These emigrants are not only Europe's most skilled workers but, according to several metrics, also the most gifted in their respective fields globally, with their "quality"—expressed in terms of educational and professional backgrounds—having significantly increased over time. In short, this is the brain drain of "la creme de la creme" (pp.195-196: also see Kaba, 2017a).

Finally, of 112,794 temporary visa holders who earned doctoral degrees from U.S. colleges and universities from 2012 to 2018, 71.7% said that they intend to stay in the United States: 57.7% of 3,090 graduates from Canada; 81.4% of 36,637 graduates from China; 86.2% of 15,201 graduates from India; 62.9% of 8,764 graduates from South Korea; 71.4% of 4,325 graduates from Taiwan; 59% of 322 graduates from Australia; 63.7% of 798 graduates from France; 56.4% of 1,281 graduates from Germany; 66.4% of 1,070 graduates from Italy; 73.7% of 833 graduates from Russia; 72.5% of 639 graduate from Greece; 64.5% of 591 graduates from Spain; 60.7% of 3,232 of graduates from Turkey; 78.6% of 294 graduates from Ukraine; 61% of 728 graduates from the United Kingdom; and 56.6% of 555 graduates from Israel ("Table 53. Doctorate recipients with temporary visas intending to stay in the United States after doctorate receipt, by country of citizenship," 2020).

## Location at the Time of Birth versus Location at the Time of Award

The availability of data for a Fellow's location at the time of award is also important because that information can be compared with the place of birth data in this study, especially for the United States to observe the differences between the number of Fellows born in a particular state and region, or a country, and the number of Fellows in that state and region, or country, at the time of the award. For example, of the four regions of the United States, the Northeast and West have more Fellows at the time of award than the number of Fellows born in each region: 343 (43.3% of 793 total Fellows born in the United States) Fellows were born in the

Northeast, but 453 (46.5% of 974 total number of Fellows located in the United States at time of award) Fellows were located in the Northeast at the time of award, and 124 (15.6% of U.S. total) Fellows were born in the West, but 269 (27.6% of U.S. total) Fellows were located in the West at the time of the award. For the South, 182 (23% of U.S. total) Fellows were born there, but 135 (13.9%% of U.S. total) Fellows were located there at the time of the award. For the Midwest region, 142 (18% of U.S. total) Fellows were born there, but 117 (12% of U.S. total) Fellows were located there at the time of the award. For individual states in the United States, three of them stand out in terms of more Fellows being located there at the time of award than were born there: New York, California, and Massachusetts. There are 173 Fellows born in New York state, but 220 Fellows were located there at the time of award; 72 Fellows were born in California, but 195 Fellows were located there at the time of award, and 55 Fellows were born in Massachusetts, but 117 Fellows were located there at the time of award (Tables 2 and 6).

On the other hand, there were 11 Fellows born in Wisconsin, but 6 Fellows were located there at the time of award; 9 born in Minnesota, but 5 at the time of award; 8 born in Missouri, but 4 at the time of award; 4 born in Nebraska, but none at the time of award; 3 born in Kansas, but 1 at the time of award; 22 born in Texas, but 14 at the time of award; 21 born in Maryland, but 16 at the time of award; 19 born in Florida, but 8 at the time of award; 14 born in Georgia, but 7 at the time of award; 9 born in Alabama, but 3 at the time of award; 7 born in South Carolina, but 1 at the time of award; 6 born in Delaware, but 1 at the time of award; 6 born in Kentucky, but 2 at the time of award; 4 born in Arkansas, but 1 at the time of award; 4 born in Oklahoma, but 2 at the time of award; and 3 born in West Virginia, but 1 at the time of award (Tables 2 and 6). The MacArthur Fellows Program also examined this phenomenon of where Fellows were born versus where they were located at the time of their award (Conrad, 2014, September 2; "Creativity on the Move," 2018, October 29; Hernandez, 2013).

The data for the year Fellows earned their highest or terminal degrees help to explain why White men are the overwhelming majority of Fellows selected especially in the first decade of the MacArthur Fellows program. As it is already obvious, earning a college degree, especially a terminal degree such as doctoral, MD, or JD, puts a candidate in a position to be selected as a Fellow. It is just in the 1970s that women and minorities were accepted into higher education institutions in significant numbers. It would therefore take significant time to earn bachelor's degrees, and especially so for terminal degrees. The data above has proven that by 2019, females in the United States had earned have higher numbers and proportions of associate, bachelor's, and master's degrees than their male counterparts. However, due primarily to immigration, more males continue to have professional and doctoral degrees than their female counterparts. This fact is because of immigrant males with temporary visas, who earn a very high number or proportion of doctoral degrees from U.S. colleges and universities.

# CHAPTER SIX

## Conclusion

This study started by discussing the contributions made by various non-governmental organizations that honor or award grants or fellowships to gifted individuals. Some of these organizations require lengthy applications, while some do not require one to apply, but will have committees that would do a confidential search for gifted individuals that they select for grants. In the United States, the MacArthur Fellows Program, established in 1981, has been awarding grants worth hundreds of thousands of dollars with no strings attached to individuals the program selects over a five-year period. Around twenty to twenty-five individuals who are either citizens or residents of the United States are eligible for the award. By 2019, the amount awarded to each fellow over a five-year period was $625,000.

The study presents a conceptual definitions section to explain the terms 'genius' and 'creative' or 'creativity'. The media and the public refer to the Fellows as geniuses, while the MacArthur Fellows Program refers to them as 'creative' or used the term 'creativity' when lamenting about them (Conrad, 2014, September 3). Some definitions of the term genius tend to include the word creative or creativity, just as definitions of creativity or creative tend to include the word genius. One common definition of the term genius is a person with "exceptional intellectual or creative power or other natural ability". One definition or explanation of the term creativity is: "Creativity is not an attribute limited to the historic 'greats'—the Darwins, the Picassos, the Hemingways. Rather, it is something anyone can use. To a large extent, creativity is a decision".

The study produced many interesting findings. For example, of the 1, 014 Fellows, Whites account for over eight out of every ten; minorities account for almost 20%; Men account for almost 63%; White men account for 51.3%; White women account for 29.1%; Black men account for 7.2%; Black women account for 5.3%; Asian men account for 3.94%; Asian women account for 1.98%; Native American women account for 0.8%, and Native American men account for 0.4 percent. Asian Americans are the youngest Fellows, while Black Fellows are the oldest. Both the youngest and oldest Fellows are White males, and the youngest female Fellow is a Black woman. The mean age for all men is 45.98 years and 45.53 years for women.

The vast majority of Fellows (78.3%) were born in the United States. Of the 793 Fellows born in the United States, 43.3% were born in the Northeast, with 173 of them born in New York State alone. Of the 220 Fellows born outside of the United States, 96 (43.6%) were born in Europe, 53 (24%) were born in Asia, 33 (15%) were born in Latin America and the Caribbean, and 14 (6.4%) were born in Africa. The first names data revealed that John appeared the most (35 or 5.5%) among men and Susan appeared the most (11 or 2.9%) among women, with all of them being White. Of the 974 Fellows located in the United States at the time of award, 453 (46.5%) were in the Northeast, with 220 in New York State alone.

Finally, of the 965 terminal or highest degrees earned by 928 Fellows, 540 (56%) are doctorates, with the PhD. accounting for 514 (53.3%). Of the 965 degrees earned, 490 (50.8%) are earned by White men, 293 (30%) are earned by White women, 60 are earned by Black men, 50 are earned by Black women, 39 are earned by Asian men, 21 are earned by Asian women, 8 are earned by Native American women and 4 are earned by Native American men. Harvard University awarded the highest proportion of degrees to MacArthur Fellows with 119, followed by Yale University with 61, UC Berkeley with 51, Columbia University with 44, and Princeton University with 41. All eight Ivy League institutions awarded 306 degrees to 300 Fellows. The 2020 U.S. News and World Report Top 25 institutions combined awarded 522 degrees (54.1% of 965 total degrees) to 514 Fellows (55.5% of 928 Fellows with degrees in this study).

The data in this study has revealed that men continue to be overrepresented among those selected as MacArthur Fellows, just as they are overrepresented among those awarded many other prizes to prominent individuals in the United States. The foreign-born data tends to contribute to this phenomenon since a high majority of them in this study are men. Some minority groups such as Black men and Asian men tend to have higher proportions of Fellows than their proportions among the adult population in the United States. Earning a doctorate especially the PhD tends to result in an individual being selected as a Fellow. Ivy League and the top 25 ranked institutions are over-represented among all MacArthur Fellows.

# References

"About MacArthur Fellows Program," 2019, November 18. MacArthur Fellows Program. Retrieved on November 18, 2019 from https://www.macfound.org/programs/fellows/strategy/.

Abramo, Giovanni., and D'Angelo, Ciriaco, Andrea. 2017. "Does Your Surname Affect the Citability or Your Publications?" *Journal of Informetrics*, 11, (1): 121-127

Alexander, Rohan., and Ward, Zachary. 2018. "Age at Arrival and Assimilation During the Age of Mass Migration," *The Journal of Economic History*, 78, (3): 904.937.

Andrews, David. 2018. "The **genius effect**: What makes one a **genius**, and who can rightly or wrongly claim the title," *Credit Management*, p26-27.

Benzon, William L. 2018, October 18. "The Genius Chronicles: Going Boldly Where None Have Gone Before," Retrieved on November 18, 2019 from https://www.academia.edu/7974651/The_Genius_Chronicles_Going_Boldly_Where_None_Have_Gone_Before

Besnard, Phillippe., and Desplanques, Guy. 2001. "Temporal Stratification of Taste: the Social Diffusion of First Names," *Revue française de sociologie*, 42:65-77

*Brinkman, Antoinette. 2010. "Sudden Genius: Creativity Explored Through Ten Extraordinary Lives," (Book Review). Library Journal, 135, (4): 124.*

Campanella, Edoardo. 2015. "Reversing the Elite Brain Drain: A First Step to Address Europe's Skills Shortage," *Journal of International Affairs*, 68, (2): 195-209.

Carneiro, Pedro., Lee, Sokbae., and Reis, Hugo. 2020. "Please Call Me John: Name Choice and the Assimilation of Immigrants in the United States, 1900-1930," *Labor Economics*, 62: 1-18.

Comenetz, Joshua. 2016, October. "Frequently Occurring Surnames in the 2000 Census," United States Census Bureau. Retrieved on January 10, 2019 from: https://www2.census.gov/topics/genealogy/2010surnames/surnames.pdf.

Conrad, Cecilia, 2017, December 6. "Does Alma Mater Really Matter? Where MacArthur 'Genius' Fellows Went to College," MacArthur Fellows Program. MacArthur Foundation. Retrieved on June 28, 2018 from:https://www.macfound.org/media/files/MacArthur_Fellows_ Program_Article_Reprint_ Does_Alma_Mater_Really_Matter _oL0ntBJ.pdf).

Conrad, Cecilia, 2014, September 3. "Mobility Among Highly Creative People: What Data About MacArthur Fellows Reveal," MacArthur Fellows Program. Retrieved on December 29, 2018 from: https://www.macfound.org/press/perspectives/mobility-among-highly-creative-people-what-new-data-about-macarthur-fellows-reveals/

Conrad, Cecilia, 2014, September 2. "Geography of Geniuses: New Data About MacArthur Fellows Shows Creative People Move More," Time Magazine. Retrieved on October 10, 2019 from: https://time.com/3225774/macarthur-fellows-genius-geography-creative-people-move-more/.

Conrad, Cecilia. 2013, September 20. "5MythsaboutMacArthur 'genius' grants," Washington Post. Retrieved on December 12, 2018 from: https://www.washingtonpost.com/opinions/five-myths-about-the-macarthur-genius-grants/2013/09/20/833963b8-213f-11e3-b73c-aab60bf735d0_story.html?utm_term=.e84ce32fcd2c

Coutu, Diane. 2007. "Picking Winners: A Conversation with MacArthur Fellows Program Director Daniel J. Socolow," Harvard Business Review, 45, (1): 121-126.

Cox, June., and Daniel, Neil. 1984. "The MacArthur Fellows Look Back," *Gifted Child Today*, 35:18-25.

"Creativity on the Move," 2018, October 29. MacArthur Fellows Program. Retrieved on October 29, 2018 from: https://www.macfound.org/maps/3/

Detlefsen, Michael. 2002, Friday, June 7, "Creation and Completeness". Logic & Philosophy of Science Colloquium. Retrieved on January 3, 2019 from: https://www.lps.uci.edu/files/colloquia/01-02/MDetlefsen.html.

Epstein, Joseph. 2013. "I Dreamed of Genius: A Consideration of the Most Elusive Human Quality," Commentary. Retrieved on July 10, 2019 from: https://www.commentarymagazine.com/articles/i-dream-of-genius/

"Fellows Location at Award," 2018, October 29. MacArthur Fellows Program. Retrieved on October 29, 2019 from: https://www.macfound.org/maps/2/.

"Fellows Location at Birth," 2018, October 29. MacArthur Fellows Program. Retrieved on October 29, 2019 from: https://www.macfound.org/maps/1/.

Gans, Herbert J. 2012. "'Whitening" and the Changing American Racial Hierarchy," *Du Bois Review*, 9, (2): 267-279.

Garber, Marjorie. 2002, December. "Our Genius Problem," The Atlantic Monthly, Retrieved on July 1, 2019 from: theatlantic.com/magazine/archive/2002/12/our-genius-problem/308435/

Goldberg, Susan. 2017. "Genius Takes Many Forms," *National Geographic*, 231, (5): p.C5.

Han, Xueying., Stocking, Galen., Gebbie, Matthew A., Appelbaum, Richard P. 2015. "Will They Stay of Will They Go? International Graduate Students and Their Decisions to Stay or Leave the U.S. upon Graduation," *PLoS ONE*, 10 (3): 1-18.

Hernandez, Lee. 2013, September 25. "11 in Region Win MacArthur Genius Grants," WNYC News. Retrieved on January 15, 2019 from:https://www.wnyc.org/story/macarthur-foundation-announces-2013-genius-fellows/

"Honey, You Got a MacArthur': Blacks Who Have Received the Coveted Genius Grant," 1997. *The Journal of Blacks in Higher Education*, 17: 66-68.

Isaacson, Walter. 2017, November 27. "The Making of Genius," *Time Magazine*, 190, (22/23): 60-67.

Kaba, Amadu Jacky. 2020. "MacArthur Fellows, 1981-2018: Gender, Race and Educational Attainment," *Sociology Mind*, 10, (2): 86-126.

Kaba, Amadu Jacky. 2019. "United States Immigration Policies in the Trump Era," *Sociology Mind*, 9, (4): 316-349.

Kaba, Amadu Jacky. 2017a. *America's 'Great Immigrants': An Analysis of Carnegie Corporation's Honorees, 2006-2015*. London: Adonis & Abbey Publishers Ltd.

Kaba, Amadu Jacky. 2017b. "Educational Attainment, Citizenship, and Black American Women in Elected and Appointed National Leadership Positions," The Review of Black Political Economy, 44, (1-2): 99-136.

Kaba, Amadu Jacky. 2016. "Conceptualizing Tolerance as Recognition: Black American Endowed and Distinguished Professors of Education in US Colleges and Universities," *Sociology Mind*, 6, (1): 1-31.

Kaba, Amadu Jacky. 2015. "Contributors to the American Sociological Review, 2010," Sociology Mind, 5, (2): 114-146.

Kaba, Amadu Jacky. 2013a. *Profile of Contributors to the American Economic Review, 2010: Human Capital Theory, Gender and Race*. Irvine, California: Scientific Research Publishing, Inc. http://file.scirp.org/pdf/PCAER_chapter_2014091914502967.pdf

Kaba, Amadu Jacky. 2013b. "Profile of Contributors to the *American Political Science Review*, 2010," 2013. *Journal of Politics and Law*, 6, (2): 54-82.

Kaba, Amadu Jacky. 2012a. "Analyzing the Anglo-American hegemony in the Times Higher Education Rankings," *Education Policy Analysis Archives*, 20, (21): 1-53.

Kaba, Amadu Jacky 2012b. "Talented Tenth: An Analysis of the 2011 Root Magazine's 100 Most Influential Young Black Americans," *International Journal of Humanities and Social Science*, 2, (5): 1-31.

Kaba, Amadu Jacky. 2009. "Demographics and Profile: The Most Cited Black Scholars in the Social Sciences, Arts and Humanities," *Journal of Pan African Studies*, 3, (2): 153-207.

Kalb, Claudia. 2017, May. "Genius," *National Geographic*, 231, (5): 30-55.

Kalist, David E., and Loe, Daniel Y. 2009. "First Names and Crime: Does Unpopularity Spell Trouble?" *Social Science Quarterly*, 90, (1): 39-49.

Kaufman, James C., and Sternberg, Robert J. 2007. "Creativity," *Resource Review*, 39, (4): 55-58.

Kinsley, Michael. 1981, June 6. "What's So Great about Excellence? Michael Kinsley on the MacArthur Grants," The New Republic, Retrieved on February 12, 2019 from: newrepublic.com/article/108017/whats-so-great-about-excellence

Lasker, Gabriel W. 1991. "Cultural Factor in the Geographic Distribution of Personal Names: Pseudogenetic Analysis of First Names Used to Estimate the Cultural Component of Coefficients of Relationship by Isonymy," Human Biology, 63, (2): 197-202

Lieberson, Stanley., and Bell, Eleanor O. 1992. "Children's First Names: An Empirical Study of Social Taste," *American Journal of Sociology*, 98, (3): 511-554.

Lubart, Todd I., and Sternberg, Robert J.1998. "Creativity Across Time and Place: Life Span and Cross-Cultural Perspectives," *High Ability Studies*, 9, (1): 59-74.

Lv, Wenpeng., and Newman Young, Barbara. 2014. "Ethnographic Research on Origins of American and Chinese Surnames," *Journal of Ethnographic & Qualitative Research*, 8, (4): 190-204.

"MacArthur Fellows Program: Summary of 2012-2013 Review," 2013. MacArthur Foundation. Retrieved on January 2020 from: https://www.macfound.org/media/files/MacArthur_Fellows_Program_Review_final_1.pdf.

MacArthur Fellows: The First 25, 1981-2005. (2005, December). The John D. and Catherine T. MacArthur Foundation. 140 South Dearborn Street. Chicago, Illinois. www.macfound.com. 410 pages.

Miller, Claire C., Quealy, Kevin., and Sanger-Katz, Margot. 2018, April 25. "The Top Jobs Where Women are Outnumbered by Men Named John," New York Times. Retrieved on January 12, 2019 from:https://www.nytimes.com/interactive/2018/04/24/upshot/women-and-men-named-john.html.

Moritz, Cynthia. 1998. "Exploring Cultural Geography," Syracuse University Magazine, 15, (1): 28-29.

"National University Rankings, 2020," 2019. U.S. News and World Report. Retrieved on November 10, 2019 from: https://www.usnews.com/best-colleges/rankings/national-universities

Orner, Rebecca. 2016. "Genius," Salem Press Encyclopedia. 5 pages.

Pais, Arthur J. 2011, September 30. "Genesis of a Genius," *India Abroad*, 20-21.

Patchett, Ann. 2017, November 22. "Tribute to Primatologist Jane Goodall," *Time Magazine*, p.64.

Pick, Grant. 1995, December 3. "The MacArthur Manner," *Chicago Tribune*, Retrieved on September 26, 2019 from: https://www.chicagotribune.com/news/ct-xpm-1995-12-03-9512030398-story.html.

Pieterse, Jan Nederveen. 1996, September. "My Paradigm or Yours? Alternative Development, Post-Development, Reflexive Development," Working Paper Series No. 229. Institute of Social Studies, The Hague, The Netherlands.

Powell, Kendall. 2008. "Best in Class," *Nature*, 455: 455–458

Raveenthiran, V. 2016. "Insensitivity of Editors and Indexers Regarding the Cultural Variations of Authos' Surnames," *BiochemiaMedica*, 6, (2):164-168.

"Review Affirms Impact and Inspiration of MacArthur Fellows Program," 2013, August 27. MacArthur Fellows Program. Retrieved on October 29, 2018 from: https://www.macfound.org/press/evaluation/macarthur-fellows-program-review-summary/.

Rocca, Alexander. 2017. "'I don't feel like a Genius'": David Foster Wallace, Trickle-Down Aesthetics, and the MacArthur Foundation," *Arizona Quarterly: A Journal of American Literature, Culture, and Theory*, 73, (1): 85-111.

Russ, Sandra W. 2016. "Pretend Play: Antecedent of Adult Creativity," New Directions for Child and Adolescent Development, 151:21-32.

Shachar, Ayelet., and Hirschl, Ran. 2013. "Recruiting "Super Talent": The New World of Selective Migration Regimes," *Indiana Journal of Global Legal Studies*, 20, (1): 71-107.

Schimke, David. 2016. "Pure Genius," *Public Art Review*, 298, (55): 38-49.

"Selected Population Profile in the United States: 2017 American Community Survey 1 Year-Estimates," 2020. American Indian and Alaska Native. American Community Survey. United States Census Bureau. https://data.census.gov/cedsci/table?d=ACS%205-Year%20Estimates%20Data%20Profiles&table=DP05&tid=ACSDP5Y2017.DP05

Silka, Linda. 2014. "Encouraging Innovation: Thoughts from Ted Ames, Prize Winner," *Maine Policy Review*, 23, (1): 82-85.

Simonton, Dean Keith. 2017. "Intellectual Genius in the Islamic Golden Age: Cross-Civilization Replications, Extensions, and Modifications," *Psychology of Aesthetics, Creativity, and the Arts*, 12, (2): 125-135.

Smirnov, Sergei D. 1994. "Intelligence and Personality in the Psychological Theory of Activity," in *Personality and Intelligence* (Edited by Robert J. Sternberg and Patricia Ruzgis). New York: Cambridge University Press. Pp. 221-245.

"Standards for the Classification of Federal Data on Race and Ethnicity," 1995, August 28.

United States *Federal Register*. Executive Office of the President of the United States

Office of Management and Budget (OMB), Office of Information and Regulatory

Affairs. Retrieved on May 1, 2013 from:obamawhitehouse.archives.gov/omb/fedreg_race-ethnicity

Starmer, C. Frank. 2013, November. "Creativists in Our Midst," Vital Science. Retrieved on January 12, 2019 from: http://www.duke.nus.edu.sg/vitalscience/201311/article-story2.html.

Sternberg, Robert J. 2012. "The Assessment of Creativity: An Investment-Based Approach," *Creativity Research Journal*, 24, (1):3-12.

Sternberg, Robert J. 2006. "The Nature of Creativity," *Creativity Research Journal*, 18, (1): 87-98.

Sternberg, Robert J. 2003. "WICS as a Model of Giftedness," *High Ability Studies*, 14, (2): 109-137.

Sternberg, Robert J., and Lubart, Todd I. 1996. "Investing in Creativity," *American Psychologist*, 51, (7): 677-688.

Stone, Chuck. 2001. "A Roster of African Americans Who Hold Endowed University Chairs," *Journal of Blacks in Higher Education*, 33: 121-125.

"Table 1. Educational Attainment of the Population 18 Years and Over, by Age, Sex, Race, and Hispanic Origin: 2019," 2020. United States Census Bureau. Retrieved on August 19, 2020 from: https://www.census.gov/data/tables/2019/demo/educational-attainment/cps-detailed-tables.html.

"Table 1. Educational Attainment of the Population 18 Years and Over, by Age, Sex, Race, and Hispanic Origin: 2018," 2019, February 21. United States Census Bureau. Retrieved on October 5, 2019 from: census.gov/data/tables/2018/demo/education-attainment/cps-detailed-tables.html.

"Table 20. Male doctorate recipients, by ethnicity, race, and citizenship status: 2009–18," 2020. Survey of Earned Doctorates. National Science Foundation (NSF). Retrieved on August 19, 2020 from: https://ncses.nsf.gov/pubs/nsf20301/data-tables.

"Table 21. Female doctorate recipients, by ethnicity, race, and citizenship status: 2009–18," 2020. Survey of Earned Doctorates. National Science Foundation (NSF). Retrieved on August 19, 2020 from: https://ncses.nsf.gov/pubs/nsf20301/data-tables.

Table 53. Doctorate recipients with temporary visas intending to stay in the United States after doctorate receipt, by country of citizenship: 2012–18," 2020. Survey of Earned Doctorates. National Science Foundation (NSF). Retrieved on August 19, 2020 from: https://ncses.nsf.gov/pubs/nsf20301/data-tables

Teich, Albert H. 2014. "Streamlining the Visa and Immigration Systems for Scientists and Engineers," *Issues in Science and Technology*, XXXI, (1): 55-64.

Torrance, E. Paul. 2004. "Great Expectations: Creative Achievements of the Sociometric Stars in a 30-Year Study," *The Journal of Secondary Gifted Education*, XVI, (1): 5-13.

Tzioumis, Konstantinos. 2018. "Demographic Aspects of First Names," Scientific Data, 5, (180025); 1-9.

Von Gunten, Charles F. 2009. "Genius," *Journal of Palliative Medicine*, 12, (1): 5.

Vorascek, Martin., Rieder, Stephan., Stieger, Stefan., and Swami, Viren. 2015. "What's in a Surname? Physique, Aptitude, and Sports Type Comparisons between Tailors and Smiths," PLoS ONE 10, (7): e0131795. 1-11.

Wallerstein, Mitchell B. 2002. "Wither the Role of Private Foundations in Support of International Security Policy," *Nonproliferation Review*, 9, (1):83–91.

Wadhwa, Vivek, A. 2009. "Reverse Brain Drain," *Issues in Science and Technology*, XXV, (3): 45-52.

Ward, F. Champion. 2001 (September/October). *"The Birth of the MacArthur Fellows Program,"* Foundation News and Commentary, 42, ( 5): 38-40.

Weisberg, Robert. 2010. "The Study of Creativity: From Genius to Cognitive Science," *International Journal of Cultural Policy*, 16, (3): 235-253.

Williams, Margaret H. 2005. "Jewish Festal Names in Antiquity – A Neglected Area of Onomastic Research," *Journal for the Study of Judaism in the Persian, Hellenistic, and Roman Period*, 36, (1): 21-40.

Wooster, Martin Morse. 2014, October 30. "Those Unassailable 'genius grants,'" Philanthropy Daily. Retrieved on July 6, 2019 from: https://www.philanthropydaily.com/those-unassailable-genius-grants/

Wooster, Martin Morse. 2010. "The MacArthur Mistake," *Commentary*, 130, (5): 39-44.

Wuffle, A., and Coulter, Kristine. 2014. "Is Political Science Meant for Every Tom, Dick, or Harriet? The Role of First Names and Middle Initials as Predictors of Academic Success," *PS: Political Science & Politics*, 47, (1): 173-176.

Yancey, George. 2003. *Who is White: Latinos, Asians, and the New Black/Nonblack Divide.*
Boulder, CO: Lynne Rienner Publishers.
Young, Julia G. 2017. "Making America 1920 Again? Nativism and US Immigration, Past and Present," *Journal of Migration and Human Security*, 5, (1): 217-235.
Young, Phillip., and Castaneda, Jos M. 2008. "Color of Money as Compared to Color of Principals: An Assessment of Pay for Male Elementary School Principals Varying in Surname (Hispanic vs. Non-Hispanic)," *Educational Administration Quarterly*, 44, (5): 675-703.
Zuckerman, Harriet, 1992. "The Proliferation of Prizes: Nobel Complements and Nobel Surrogates in the Reward System of Science," *Theoretical Medicine*, 13, (2): 217-231.
"2019 MacArthur Fellows," 2019. MacArthur Fellows Program.
Retrieved on November 23, 2019 from: https://www.macfound.org/programs/fellows/

# Appendices

## *Appendix A. Regional Breakdown of the United States (N = 51)*

Northeast (n = 9) Connecticut, Maine, Massachusetts, New Hampshire, New Jersey, New York, Pennsylvania, Rhode Island, Vermont.
Midwest (n = 12) Illinois, Indiana, Iowa, Kansas, Michigan, Minnesota, Missouri, Nebraska, North, Dakota, Ohio, South Dakota, Wisconsin.
South (n = 17) Alabama, Arkansas, Delaware, District of Columbia, Florida, Georgia, Kentucky, Louisiana, Maryland, Mississippi, North Carolina, Oklahoma, South Carolina, Tennessee, Texas, Virginia, West Virginia.
West (n = 13) Alaska, Arizona, California, Colorado, Hawaii, Idaho, Montana, Nevada, New Mexico, Oregon, Utah, Washington, Wyoming.
Source: "Summary Social, Economic, and Housing Characteristics: 2000 Census of Population and Housing," (2003, June). Selected Appendixes: 2000. PHC-2-A. Washington, D.C.: U.S. Census Bureau.

**Appendix B. Composition of macro geographical (continental) regions, geographical sub-regions, and selected economic and other groupings Nations, Territories and Entities plus Taiwan (N = 239).**

**Africa (N = 58)**
**Eastern Africa** (n = 20): Burundi, Comoros, Djibouti, Eritrea, Ethiopia, Kenya, Madagascar, Malawi, Mauritius, Mayotte, Mozambique, Reunion, Rwanda, Seychelles, Somalia, South Sudan, Tanzania, Uganda, Zambia, and Zimbabwe.
**Middle Africa (n = 9):** Angola, Cameroon, Central African Republic, Chad, Republic of Congo, Democratic Republic of Congo, Equatorial Guinea, Gabon and Sao Tome & Principe.
**Northern Africa (n = 7):** Algeria, Egypt, Libya, Morocco, Sudan, Tunisia and Western Sahara. Southern Africa (n = 5) Botswana, Lesotho, Namibia, South Africa and Swaziland.
**Western Africa (n = 17):** Benin, Burkina Faso, Cape Verde, Cote d'Ivoire, The Gambia, Ghana, Guinea, Guinea-Bissau, Liberia, Mali, Mauritania, Niger, Nigeria, Senegal, Sierra Leone, Togo and Saint Helena.
**Americas N = 53**
**Latin America and the Caribbean (n = 48):**
**Caribbean (n = 26):** Anguilla, Antigua and Barbuda, Aruba, Bahamas, Barbados, British Virgin Islands, Cayman Islands, Cuba, Dominica, Dominican Republic, Grenada, Guadeloupe, Haiti, Jamaica, Martinique, Montserrat, Netherlands Antilles, Puerto Rico, Saint-Barthélemy, Saint Kitts and Nevis, Saint Lucia, Saint Martin (French part), Saint Vincent and the Grenadines, Trinidad and Tobago, Turks and Caicos Islands, United States Virgin Islands.
**Central America (n = 8):** Belize, Costa Rica, El Salvador, Guatemala, Honduras, Mexico, Nicaragua, Panama.
**South America (n = 14):** Argentina, Bolivia (Plurinational State of), Brazil, Chile, Colombia, Ecuador, Falkland Islands (Malvinas), French Guiana, Guyana, Paraguay, Peru, Suriname, Uruguay, Venezuela (Bolivarian Republic of).
**Northern America (n = 5):** Bermuda, Canada, Greenland, Saint Pierre and Miquelon, United States of America.
**Asia (n = 51)**

**Central Asia (n = 5)**:Kazakhstan, Kyrgyzstan, Tajikistan, Turkmenistan, Uzbekistan.
**Eastern Asia (n = 8):** China, Hong Kong Special Administrative Region of China, Macao Special Administrative Region of China, Democratic People's Republic of Korea, Japan, Mongolia, Republic of Korea, Taiwan* (As noted in the methodology, I added Taiwan to Eastern Asia).
**Southern Asia (n = 9):** Afghanistan, Bangladesh, Bhutan, India, Iran (Islamic Republic of), Maldives, Nepal, Pakistan, Sri Lanka.
**South-Eastern Asia (n = 11):** Brunei Darussalam, Cambodia, Indonesia, Lao People's Democratic Republic, Malaysia, Myanmar, Philippines, Singapore, Thailand, Timor-Leste, Viet Nam.
**Western Asia (n = 18):** Armenia, Azerbaijan, Bahrain, Cyprus, Georgia, Iraq, Israel, Jordan, Kuwait, Lebanon, Occupied Palestinian Territory (Gaza and the West Bank), Oman, Qatar, Saudi Arabia, Syrian Arab Republic, Turkey, United Arab Emirates, Yemen.
**Europe (N = 52)**
**Eastern Europe (n = 10):** Belarus, Bulgaria, Czech Republic, Hungary, Poland, Republic of Moldova, Romania, Russian Federation, Slovakia, Ukraine.
**Northern Europe (n = 17)**:Åland Islands, Channel Islands, Denmark, Estonia, Faeroe Islands, Finland, Guernsey, Iceland, Ireland, Isle of Man, Jersey, Latvia, Lithuania, Norway, Svalbard and Jan Mayen Islands, Sweden, United Kingdom of Great Britain and Northern Ireland.
**Southern Europe (n = 16):** Albania, Andorra, Bosnia and Herzegovina, Croatia, Gibraltar, Greece, Holy See, Italy, Malta, Montenegro, Portugal, San Marino, Serbia, Slovenia, Spain, The former Yugoslav Republic of Macedonia.
**Western Europe (n = 9):** Austria, Belgium, France, Germany, Liechtenstein, Luxembourg, Monaco, Netherlands, Switzerland.
**Oceania (N = 25):**
**Australia and New Zealand (n = 3):** Australia, New Zealand, Norfolk Island.
**Melanesia (n = 5):** Fiji, New Caledonia, Papua New Guinea, Solomon Islands, Vanuatu.
**Micronesia (n = 7)**: Guam, Kiribati, Marshall Islands, Micronesia (Federated States of), Nauru, Northern Mariana Islands, Palau.

**Polynesia (n=10)**: American Samoa, Cook Islands, French Polynesia, Niue, Pitcairn, Samoa, Tokelau, Tonga, Tuvalu, Wallis and Futuna Islands.

Source: "Composition of macro geographical (continental) regions, geographical sub-regions, and selected economic and other groupings" Retrieved on January 29, 2019 from: https://unstats.un.org/unsd/methodology/m49/.

# Index

## A

Alabama, 26, 29, 79, 110, 124
*American Political Science Review*, 96, 118
*American Sociological Review*, 96, 104, 118
Anthropologists, 19
Archaeologists, 19
Architects, 19
Argentina, 27, 28, 89, 125
Arizona State University, 19, 82
Artists, 8, 17, 19
Asian ancestry, 21
Atlantic Ocean, 109
Attorneys, 19
Australia, 7, 27, 29, 30, 59, 73, 89, 108, 109, 126
Authors, 19, 35

## B

Biologists, 19
Boston University, 19, 74
Brazil, 27, 28, 125
Brown University, 7, 19, 76, 103, 104, 105, 106, 107

## C

California, 11, 19, 22, 26, 28, 29, 30, 59, 71, 72, 82, 83, 105, 106, 107, 110, 118, 124
Cambodia, 30, 126
Caribbean, 27, 28, 29, 73, 89, 114, 125
Chile, 27, 28, 89, 125
China, 11, 21, 27, 28, 30, 85, 98, 100, 102, 108, 109, 125
City University of New York, 19, 72
Columbia University, 7, 11, 19, 72, 75, 103, 104, 105, 106, 107, 114
Côte d'Ivoire, 7
Czechoslovakia, 27, 29, 102

## D

Dartmouth College, 7, 74, 103, 104, 105, 106, 107
Denmark, 27, 87, 102, 126
Doctor of Medicine degrees, 18

## E

Eastern Europe, 27, 29
*Edison, Thomas A.*, 15
Europe, 10, 11, 21, 27, 28, 59, 72, 86, 87, 88, 99, 109, 114, 115, 126

## G

Germany, 7, 27, 28, 88, 102, 108, 109, 126
Ghana, 27, 29, 125
Greece, 27, 29, 102, 109, 126

## H

Hartley Avenue, 103
Harvard University, 7, 11, 19, 72, 74, 103, 104, 105, 106, 107, 114
Hispanic, 55, 95, 121, 123
**Hungary**, 86, 102, 126

## I

India, 11, 21, 27, 30, 98, 100, 101, 108, 109, 119, 125
Indiana University, 19, 77
Italy, 27, 29, 87, 102, 109, 126
Ivy League universities, 7

## J

Japan, 7, 11, 21, 27, 30, 85, 98, 100, 102, 125
Juris Doctorate, 18, 104

## L

Latin America, 27, 28, 59, 73, 89, 114, 125
Latvia, 27, 28, 126

## M

MacArthur Fellows Program, 8, 9, 10, 13, 16, 18, 19, 20, 21, 22, 23, 26, 35, 44, 53, 54, 58, 65, 69, 90, 93, 96, 110, 113, 115, 116, 117, 119, 120, 122, 123
Massachusetts Institute of Technology, 20, 72, 74, 105, 106
Middle East, 21

## N

Native American men, 25, 65, 66, 67, 70, 71, 73, 90, 91, 113, 114
Netherlands, 7, 27, 28, 119, 125, 126
*New York Times*, 22, 101, 119
New Zealand, 27, 29, 108, 126
Nobel Memorial Prize, 8
North Africa, 21
Northern Africa, 27, 28, 29, 85, 98, 125

## O

Oceania, 27, 29, 30, 59, 73, 89, 126
One-Thousand-Talent program, 108

## P

Pakistan, 11, 21, 27, 30, 100, 125
Philippines, 21, 30, 126
Poland, 27, 29, 86, 102, 126
Princeton University, 7, 11, 20, 72, 74, 103, 104, 105, 106, 107, 114

## S

Simon, Lateefah, 22

Socolow, Daniel J, 96, 116
South Korea, 21, 30, 98, 108, 109
Spain, 27, 29, 102, 109, 126
Sri Lanka, 21, 125
Standards for the Classification of Federal Data on Race and Ethnicity, 20, 120
Switzerland, 27, 88, 126

## T

Thailand, 21, 126
*Times Higher Education*, 7, 118
Traore, Karim, ii
Tunisia, 27, 28, 99, 125
Turkey, 21, 28, 98, 109, 126

## U

Ukraine, 27, 29, 86, 109, 126
United Kingdom, 7, 27, 28, 87, 104, 108, 109, 126
University of California, Berkeley, 11, 20, 72, 83, 105, 106
University of Pennsylvania, 7, 20, 72, 76, 103, 104, 105, 106, 107

## V

Vanderbilt University, 20, 81, 105, 106

## W

Washington, D.C., 26, 28, 29, 59, 81, 124
Western Africa, 27, 29, 85, 125
White House Office of Management and Budget, 20
World Factbook, 7

## Y

Yale University, 7, 11, 20, 72, 73, 103, 104, 105, 106, 107, 114

www.ingramcontent.com/pod-product-compliance
Lightning Source LLC
Chambersburg PA
CBHW032301150426
43195CB00008BA/538